OF INCREDIBLE

Finding Your Promised Land
When the Odds Seem Stacked Against You

Sam Rowland

ON THE EDGE OF INCREDIBLE
Copyright © 2020 by Sam Rowland

Unless otherwise indicated, all Scripture quotations are taken from the Holy Bible, New Living Translation, copyright © 1996, 2004, 2015 by Tyndale House Foundation. Used by permission of Tyndale House Publishers, a Division of Tyndale House Ministries, Carol Stream, Illinois 60188. All rights reserved. Scripture quotations marked (AMP) taken from the Amplified® Bible (AMP), Copyright © 2015 by The Lockman Foundation Used by permission. www. Lockman.org. Scripture quotations marked MSG are taken from THE MESSAGE, copyright © 1993, 2002, 2018 by Eugene H. Peterson. Used by permission of NavPress. All rights reserved. Represented by Tyndale House Publishers, a Division of Tyndale House Ministries. Scripture quotations are from the ESV® Bible (The Holy Bible, English Standard Version®), copyright © 2001 by Crossway, a publishing ministry of Good News Publishers. Used by permission. All rights reserved. Scripture quotations marked (ERV) taken from the HOLY BIBLE: EASY-TO-READ VERSION © 2001 by World Bible Translation Center, Inc. and used by permission. Scripture quotations marked (TLB) are taken from The Living Bible copyright © 1971. Used by permission of Tyndale House Publishers, a Division of Tyndale House Ministries, Carol Stream, Illinois 60188. All rights reserved. Scripture quotations marked (NIV) are taken from the Holy Bible, New International Version®, NIV®. Copyright © 1973, 1978, 1984, 2011 by Biblica, Inc.® Used by permission of Zondervan. All rights reserved worldwide. www.zondervan.com The "NIV" and "New International Version" are trademarks registered in the United States Patent and Trademark Office by Biblica, Inc.®

Printed in Canada

ISBN: 978-1-4866-2053-1
eBook ISBN: 978-1-4866-2054-8

Word Alive Press
119 De Baets Street Winnipeg, MB R2J 3R9
www.wordalivepress.ca

Cataloguing in Publication information can be obtained from Library and Archives Canada.

*This book is dedicated to every person who,
even in the midst of their daily challenges,
dares to step forward into
undiscovered joy.*

ACKNOWLEDGEMENTS

Special thanks to Brad and Wendi Eizenga, Jeanne Weber, Paul and Janet Craig, Dale and Darice Lutz, Joyce Dodds, Karl and Wendy Janzen, Gloria Riemer, John and Marianne Rissling, Evan Braun, Jen Jandavs-Hedlin, and the whole crew at Word Alive Press. Additional thanks to our incredible team of friends and partners who stand with us in so many wonderful ways—you know who you are!

CONTENTS

INTRODUCTION

The other day, I was trying to get out the door and run some errands. Just one problem: the car keys weren't in their usual place.

So I started searching. I searched my night table drawers. I searched in the kitchen. I turned the garage inside-out looking for those keys. In fact, I tore the whole house upside-down. Nowhere.

I even questioned my wife, somewhat suspiciously, implying that this predicament might just be her responsibility.

Imagine my embarrassment when, while washing my hands in front of the bathroom mirror, I noticed that right over my own beating heart my shirt pocket had a key-fob-shaped bulge in it.

That's right. I'd had the key with me the whole time.

I've got some great news for you right off the top: your key is within reach, too. You are much closer than you think to living a life that deeply satisfies your heart and soul, even if it *feels* like that's not true for you right now. In fact, for many people, it *feels* impossible. It might even *look* impossible.

In spite of our feelings and perspectives, though, it is still absolutely, undeniably true: you are living on the edge of incredible. You're receiving an invitation in these very words—an invitation to more freedom than you've ever thought possible. It's an invitation to revel in unconditional acceptance, to make a positive impact in the lives of those around you, and to move past the edge of incredible right to the very centre.

Just like that key fob in my shirt pocket, the answers you're looking for, the freedom you're longing for, even the relationships you were made for, are all much closer than you might realize.

Instead of turning your whole world upside-down in search of your promised land, you may discover that what you're longing for is already very close to your heart.

I want to warn you, though: in order to discover these precious assets, you may be invited to move in a direction that could feel frightening. Vulnerability may be required, even in your relationship with yourself. If your comfort zone is more important to you than the future you've dreamed about, please stop reading now.

But if you're hungry for more, if you know in your bones that you were made for more, then read on.

I have two questions for you. Do you love to lose yourself in a grand adventure on the big screen as you simultaneously soak in the incredible soundtrack? And if so, are you ready to begin experiencing your own adventure now, with a soundtrack tailored to you and your life?

As the pieces of your puzzle fall into place, you'll begin to see the bigger picture take shape. You may be surprised to see how your story, even your deepest wounds, have helped to prepare you for discovering more life than you ever thought possible. Along this journey, you will have opportunities to choose between steps of fear and steps of faith.

And if you dare to take courageous and vulnerable steps of faith, you'll discover that the life you've been seeking is truly within your reach.

In this brief book, I'm going to be vulnerable with you. I only ask that you consider being vulnerable with yourself as well. You'll be amazed at the doors which will be unlocked by the keys that are, even in this moment, waiting patiently to be discovered.

One

LYRICS TO A LOVE SONG

Sometimes I want to get close to God, but even after all these years of Him loving me, I'm still so afraid of rejection.

Fortunately, I sometimes choose to ignore my fear.

A few weeks ago, I chose not only to come near to God but to expose my heart to Him. Now I realize that He sees all of me all the time, but it's still—at least for me—intimidating to choose to make myself vulnerable to Him.

I have a little journal in which I write some of my thoughts and prayers. On that particular day, I wrote and spoke these words from my heart to God's heart:

> Lord, what do You want to prune in my life, or what do
> You want to make me aware of?

Well, knowing my own heart, I braced myself for a barrage of judgments and guilty verdicts from which I might never recover. In fact, that's probably exactly what I deserved.

But that morning, I didn't get what I deserved.

I wrote down the words that settled gently on me:

I want to prune dissatisfaction, disharmony, fear, discouragement, and judgment from your life.

But He didn't stop with what He wanted to prune. He continued with what He wanted to graft, to implant and splice into my life:

I want you to rediscover abundant acceptance, a sense of well-being, overflowing hope, and the rock-solid foundation that you have in Me.

I invite you to reread the two sentences above slowly, letting the flavour of the words drip over your life.

These aren't just words. These are the lyrics to a love song. And based on the whole of Scripture, I can confidently declare that God is singing this love song over your life today.

The Old Testament prophet Zephaniah puts it this way:

For the Lord your God is living among you. He is a mighty savior. He will take delight in you with gladness. With his love, he will calm all your fears. He will rejoice over you with joyful songs. (Zephaniah 3:17)

If we're willing to humble ourselves and seek His face, we'll be able to hear those joyful songs. At first they'll be faint strains, but don't give up. In our brokenness, in our most vulnerable moments, we have the best opportunity to move forward.

Unfortunately, if we're pretty darned confident that we're better than others and close to getting it right all by ourselves, we won't want to hear this song. Why? Because we haven't earned it and we can't take any pride in it.

If you're anything like me, though, you know that you're not even close to earning it and never, ever will be. And yet the Lord wants to sing His song over you because of the undeserved kindness He wants to pour over your life.

A little girl named Emma was once asked for her definition of love in a Grade One school assignment. She responded, "Love is when you're missing some of your teeth, but you're not afraid to smile, because you know your friends will love you even though some of you is missing."[1]

God loves you like that.

---

[1] Leah Sheitel, "A Smile Is Greater than the Sum of its Teeth: Planting to Pay the Dentist," *Brinkman Group*. Date of access: August 9, 2020 (http://www.brinkmanforest.com/news/smile-greater-sum-its-teeth).

TWO
BIG PROMISES

If the creator of the universe wanted to do something very special in your life today, would you consider letting Him?

Even if you don't believe in a creator of the universe, just imagine for a moment that He or She might exist. If there was a loving Father who made you, would you be even remotely open to receiving His gift for you today?

Finally, if the Lord—if He or She existed—asked about your availability to be launched into a beautiful new reality as you read this book, how would you respond?

Some of the people holding this book today are in the best place they've ever been in their whole lives. Others are more broken-hearted than they ever believed possible. Most of us are somewhere in between.

I've been through a few of these different seasons myself, and so have you. Are you walking beside a stream of abundance right now? Or perhaps you're walking through the wilderness in a desert place you never planned to visit.

In any case, I want to share something very important with you. This will relate to your specific personal situation no matter what season you find yourself in, whether you feel like you're on top of the world or you can barely think about living another day.

The truth is that right in this unique moment and right in your particular location, you're living on the edge of incredible. Not only that, but before you finish this book you will clearly see how and why you're living there. You'll also meet others on these pages who will inspire you to see new possibilities unfolding right in front of you.

Additionally, you'll have the opportunity to move beyond the *edge* of incredible and right into the *centre*. You'll have the latitude to travel into new spaces that grant you access to more freedom, more joy, and more life than you've ever experienced before.

Big promises? Absolutely. And you can hold me to them.

Three
DEFINING INCREDIBLE

For the purposes of clarity, what is our definition of *incredible?* It's very simple and straightforward. One definition goes like this: "so extraordinary as to seem impossible."[2] Do you want a second opinion? Another says that the word means "amazing; astonishing; awe-inspiring."[3]

Don't believe me? Look it up for yourself.

I've got some really transformational news for every person reading these words: even if this is the toughest day you've ever experienced, your life is still on the edge of incredible. Your life is on the verge of being so wonderful as to make it seem impossible. You're also on the brink of things that are amazing, astonishing, and awe-inspiring.

Does that mean it's going to be pain-free? No. Does that mean it's going to be easy? Definitely not.

Do you know who comes to mind when I talk about this?

[2] *Dictionary.com*, "Incredible." Date of access: July 29, 2020 (https://www.dictionary.com/browse/incredible).

[3] *Definitions.net*, "Incredible." Date of access: July 29, 2020 (https://www.definitions.net/definition/incredible).

The Apostle Paul in prison, while he was writing much of what would one day become the New Testament, the part of the Bible written shortly after Jesus came to the earth.

Were Paul's life circumstances exactly what he wanted them to be? Nope. Was he in the season of life he wanted to be in? Probably not. Was he in the highly rated hotel suite he had checked out on hotels.com? No way. He was in a Roman prison.

Yet the Apostle Paul was living not just on the edge of incredible, but in the very centre of it.

A few years ago, I wrote and recorded a song called "You Are My Life." In the second verse of that song, the lyrics say,

I don't need to be afraid
I can live my life and come what may
Though the mountains fall in the sea
Cause my life is built on higher ground
Than any mountains ever found
And because I know you walk each step with me

It's pretty easy to sing these words. But can you imagine how it would change our lives if we allowed them to be true in our hearts and minds? I wrote this song based on Psalm 46:1–3, which says,

God is our refuge and strength, always ready to help in times of trouble. So we will not fear when earthquakes come and the mountains crumble into the sea. Let the oceans roar and foam. Let the mountains tremble as the waters surge!

I think the writer was basically trying to say that even if the worst possible thing happened, the earth caving in on itself, we don't need to be afraid. If it includes the world caving in on itself, I would dare say this "not fearing" thing includes all the issues happening in our lives right now, no matter how difficult they are.

You might say to yourself, *How can my life be on the edge of something good, Sam? You see, I haven't told anyone, but the doctors have told me I have cancer.* Or maybe you're thinking, *Only my spouse and I know that our marriage is as good as dead.* Or, *If only you knew how anxious I felt at times, afraid to even be around people.*

But I would come back to you and say, yes, you're on the very knife's edge right now. No matter what you're facing, you have the opportunity to abandon yourself into the strong arms of God.

I can pretty much guarantee that it'll be hard, and at times along the journey you will be broken-hearted. But you can break through that and get beyond it. You can capture a new vision for life on the other side of the raging river, for a life in your promised land.

Four
FACING YOUR GREATEST FEAR

A few years ago, I had the privilege of visiting the stunningly beautiful island nation of Mauritius, just off the coast of Madagascar. One afternoon we travelled by car to the southwestern part of the island to experience Le Morne, a most impressive mountain peninsula that dominates the landscape by air, land, and sea. Its summit of cliffs tower more than five hundred and fifty metres over the Indian Ocean.

My Mauritian friend explained to me that in the 1800s, slaves sometimes ran away from their masters' homes and came to Le Morne to hide in the mountaintop caves. This was their only alternative to shackles and beatings.

Unbeknownst to those frightened slaves-in-hiding, on February 1, 1835, slavery was abolished by the British colonial powers ruling over Mauritius at that time. The slaves instantaneously became free women and men, their whole lives ahead of them.

There was only one problem: they didn't realize they were free. Though they were as autonomous as anyone else in the country, they still had the mindset of slaves.

A group of policemen was assigned to climb the mountain and let these people know that the slavery laws had been abolished, to inform them that they no longer needed to live under fear and tyranny.

When these newly freed slaves saw the police climbing the mountain trail, they feared the very worst. They were so filled with hopelessness and dread that they threw themselves off the cliffs of Le Morne en masse. Instead of taking a step of faith towards the new life before them, they took a step of fear, from five hundred and fifty metres up.

More than their dreams were dashed on the rocks below on that heart-breaking February morning in 1835.

But their story is not your story.

There have been times in my life when, like the former slaves of Mauritius, I saw absolutely no hope for my future. Perhaps you feel that way at times as well. It's not at all uncommon. But it doesn't have to stay that way if you want something more.

Maybe you're feeling a little more positive than that, but too many days are kind of blah and you wonder why. We've all had our fair share of those days, too, but should it really be the norm?

Normal means putting our full trust in our feelings and perspectives. But is it possible we need to *reset* normal in order to help us discover our unique role in this brief life we have been given?

Too many people live as though they are slaves, hiding in dark and lonely caves of isolation. They believe their choices are limited, their value conditional, and their future laughable. I used to believe that about myself.

Used to.

The Book of Proverbs presents a series of ancient writings, and one verse in particular contains thirteen words that have the capacity to change your life. Are you ready for them? As you read these thirteen words, I want you to keep in mind the Mauritian slaves who ended their own lives.

Okay, here they are: *"Above all, be careful what you think because your thoughts control your life"* (Proverbs 4:23, ERV).

It was true of the Mauritian slaves, and it's true of every successful and unsuccessful person in the world. It's true of both you and me.

Dr. Edith Eger, holocaust survivor and author of *The Choice*, says, "To change our behaviour... we must change our feelings, and to change our feelings, we change our thoughts."[4]

But how do we change our thoughts in order to change our feelings in order to change our behaviours? The Apostle Paul wrote, *"[L]et God transform you into a new person by changing the way you think. Then you will learn to know God's will for you, which is good and pleasing and perfect"* (Romans 12:2).

I don't know about you, but the idea of having God's plan for my life come to pass is pretty appealing—His good, pleasing, and perfect will. Even if it's tough at times, I know He and I can do this together.

I also know that the same great invitation is waiting for you. You may think to yourself, *This all sounds great. I really don't want to let fear hold me back from all the very best, and I want to take steps of faith, not fear—but how do I even begin to know God or let God transform me into a new person by changing the way I think?*

One day many years ago, I was at the lowest point of my life. I felt like a slave to disappointment and hopelessness. I was

---

[4] Dr. Edith Eger, *The Choice* (New York, NY: Simon & Schuster, 2017), 171.

actually considering taking that leap of fear in order to end the pain of my aching heart.

And then God whispered in my ear, *"When you come looking for me, you'll find me. Yes, when you get serious about finding me and want it more than anything else, I'll make sure you won't be disappointed... I'll turn things around for you"* (Jeremiah 29:13–14, MSG).

Every single day, we're faced with making decisions and taking steps of fear or faith. We all have our own Le Mornes to deal with. For some, it's the possible end of a marriage or the breakup of a family. For others, it's a financial crisis. For yet others, it's an unexpected critical diagnosis from the doctor.

It can feel like we're facing the end, or at least the end as we know it. We're full of fear and dread and we've lost all hope for life beyond the loss.

But this is, in fact, the time when you're closest to a breakthrough, because this is when you're finally ready to get serious about finding a living relationship with your creator. When you want that more than anything else, He will meet you in that broken, painful, and barren place.

As Jesus said, *"A thief is only there to steal and kill and destroy. I came so they can have real and eternal life, more and better life than [you] ever dreamed of"* (John 10:10, MSG).

I'm not here to tell you that God will take all your problems away. In fact, I'm pretty sure that He won't. I'm not even here to tell you that your life will be easy and carefree.

What I'm here to tell you is that He can change your mind and your heart, and even if the circumstances of your life remain the same, that change of your mind and heart will change *everything*.

Five

BRING YOUR FEAR AND LEAVE IT HERE

Of course, you can't see me as I'm writing these words to you—but if you could, you'd see that my hiking backpack is sitting on the floor beside my desk. I'm not wearing it, because that would be stupid. It's got thirty-five or forty pounds of stuff in it! Why would I carry all that around in my day-to-day life? The backpack is useful for carrying special supplies on specific journeys.

As I write these words, most of my friends and I are looking forward to a football game this afternoon. A big game.

Here's a question for you: would you want your team's star player to have a forty-pound backpack on his shoulders? I mean, how would that affect him? He wouldn't be able to fulfill his destiny, right? It would be moronic; it would be crazy! He wouldn't even be able to keep up with the slowest players on the field.

And yet what do you carry in your backpack 24/7 that keeps you from living the life God created you to live?

I recently took some extra one-on-one time with God. Now, you might think that missionaries and pastors spend a lot of time with God, that they're so holy, but we're more human than most, believe me.

On this particular day, though, I really sought God's face. I said, "God, if there's a message You want me to share with the people You created, what would that message be?"

This is the phrase that came deep to my heart: "Bring your fear and leave it here."

God is in the business of lifting us up. He's not in the business of putting heavy weights on our back and making us go through life carrying the heavy burden.

Some so-called religious people may want to do that to you, though. In Matthew 23:3–4, Jesus speaks of the religious leaders of His day, saying, *"[D]on't follow their example. For they don't practice what they teach. They crush people with unbearable religious demands and never lift a finger to ease the burden."* Jesus will never do that to you. In fact, He does just the opposite—if we let Him.

Do we have heavy weights to deal with in this life? Yes, we absolutely do. Are we meant to carry them ourselves? No, we absolutely are not.

Some of us are still carrying around our sins and mistakes from decades ago. Instead we need to say, "No more. Jesus died for this. He died so I could be free. No matter how difficult or awful I was, it's time to let it go. Today is the first day of my freedom."

In Hebrews 8:12, the Lord says, *"And I will forgive their wickedness, and I will never again remember their sins."* It was author and speaker Joyce Meyer who said, "Stop remembering what God has forgotten!"[5]

---

[5] Joyce Meyer, "Stop remembering what God has forgotten," *Twitter.* November 22, 2016 (https://twitter.com/joycemeyer/status/801108426969542656?lang=en).

Six
1.3 BILLION PEOPLE

Recently I was invited to visit Chennai, a city on the central -eastern coast of the beautiful, mysterious, and very populous country of India. More than 1.3 billion people call India home! While I love people very much, I'm not so great with huge crowds. It's not so strong a discomfort as to be called a phobia, but I love the freedom to move around and have a large, Canadian-sized personal space bubble!

I've heard people talk about being overwhelmed as they landed in India and walked out of the airport for the very first time. The Canadian comic Russell Peters, a man born in Canada of Indian descent, said he was stunned by the experience. Because of this, I was more than just a little bit anxious as I collected my bags, walked through customs, and stepped out into the warm and humid midnight air.

In India, only travellers themselves are allowed to enter the airport. Family and friends must wait outside with hundreds, and sometimes thousands, of other people, everyone hoping to catch a glimpse of their loved ones as they call out their names above the din of the crowd.

Though I had come to India by invitation, I had never even met the man who had invited me. We had only traded emails and had three very brief phone calls. In fact, though I knew many Indians living in Canada, I hadn't previously met even one of these 1.3 billion people before!

A few days in advance of my journey, I called the hotel where I would be staying for my first two nights in India. They told me that if I emailed them all my flight details, someone would pick me up at the airport.

As I walked out of the airport after twenty-two hours of travel, I was a little overwhelmed. I scanned the crowd gathered there, and just before I reached the crush of the multitudes I saw a smiling man holding up a sign that said "SAM ROWLAND."

My anxiety instantly dissipated. In a land of untold millions, somebody knew my name! Not only that, but before I knew or cared about this man, he had prepared to come and receive me. As I had been journeying to India, this man had left the comfort of his home in the middle of the night to come and welcome me, and then deliver me to the exact place I needed to be.

As we journey through this life, we're all heading towards eternity. In the midst of it all, the creator God is reaching out to us. Before we knew or cared about God, He was making a plan for our good. In fact, before we knew or cared about Him, Jesus left His home to come to this earth. John 3:16–18 in The Message paraphrase puts it this way:

This is how much God loved the world: He gave his Son, his one and only Son. And this is why: so that no one need be destroyed; by believing in him, anyone can have a whole and lasting life. God didn't go to all the trouble of sending his Son merely to point an accusing finger, telling the world how bad it was. He came to help, to put the world right again. Anyone who trusts in him is acquitted. (MSG)

Do you worry sometimes that God has forgotten you, or that it's too late for you? The Lord knows our deepest fears, so He reassures us by saying, *"Can a mother forget her nursing child? Can she feel no love for the child she has borne? But even if that were possible, I would not forget you!"* (Isaiah 49:15)

But the Lord doesn't stop there. Read these next words slowly to let them sink in: *"See, I have written your name on the palms of my hands"* (Isaiah 49:16).

Imagine, our names are written on the palms of God's hands! When we leave this life on earth, we won't find a hotel employee with a printed sign containing our name; it will be the living God holding out His hands to us, and our name will be written there. Unbelievable!

I guess it's just about as unbelievable as it would have been for the Mauritian slaves who had been made free. Let's just not make the same mistake they did.

This truth helps my anxiety to fall as I sense a strong and fresh wind beginning to fill the sails of my faith journey.

Seven

ARE YOU READY TO LIGHTEN YOUR LOAD?

Some people feel very afraid of the future. Just the thought of it puts a knot in their stomach. They're trading today's joy for tomorrow's worries. Not a good trade at all.

I met a wonderful young man recently who has a great heart for the Lord, and he believes the Lord is calling him overseas. But as he shared his heart with me, he said, "I have one issue that will really get in the way."

"Would you be willing to let the Lord take care of that issue?" I asked.

It turns out he's got some heavy fear in his backpack. He won't make the journey successfully if he keeps carrying that heavy weight on his back.

How about you? Are you ready to lighten your load? Today—right now, in fact—you will be given the opportunity to bring your fear to your creator and leave it at His feet. You're going to have the opportunity to bend your knee at the place of grace, that place where your heart becomes intimately interconnected with God's heart. You're invited to lay whatever's in your backpack, whatever's holding you back from being freer than you've ever been before, at the feet of the living God.

As we look at someone else, they might seem successful, like they've got it all together. Yet you have no idea what they're carrying. They might have one of those heavy backpacks, too. Everyone carries one at some time or another.

My growing up years were so awful, some of us think. *I'm never going to do that to my kids. I'm going to be the perfect parent and do what my parents couldn't do for me.*

And we fill our backpack with these anxieties.

You're carrying a burden that isn't yours to carry. If you truly want to be free, you can say to God, "Father, I went through some really hard times that hurt me and left some wounds. I'm going to lay this at Your feet and trust You to do what needs to be done in my heart, in my life, and in my family. Please heal this wound. It's okay if it leaves a scar, but Lord, heal this seeping wound."

It could be your finances, or it could be some other type of anxiety. Everyone reading this book has something to deal with, but God's amazing grace is enough for each of us.

Perhaps your parents divorced when you were younger and now you're putting a lot of pressure on yourself to make your marriage work. You're holding on to it as a heavy weight in your backpack.

Instead, you can say to God, "I'll do what You ask me to do. I'll love how You ask me to love. But I'm not going to carry the burden of this. I will trust You with this broken part of my life. I will trust You with this broken part of my heart."

Eight

WHEN IT HURTS TOO MUCH

When I was fifteen years old, my family fell apart. My parents went in different directions and we kids were torn into two camps. It was the most broken and fragmented period of my life, full of hopelessness and pain. My emotions told me to stop the pain by stopping my heart from beating. I had to decide whether to kill myself.

But in that season, I was on the edge of incredible. I had the opportunity to abandon myself to God.

I fell on my knees one evening and sobbed and sobbed. I was with a group of kids from a church youth group, and they gathered around me and put their hands on my shoulders. They prayed over me. They prayed *for* me. They trusted God on my behalf for what I was too weak and broken to trust God for.

Did the Lord take away all my pain that night? Not at all. Did He solve the problem? Not to my liking. But did everything change?

Yes.

I collapsed into His strong arms and said, "God, I'm at the end of myself. I can't carry this anymore. I'm giving this to You."

I didn't just trust God with my pain for a few weeks or a few months. It was years—years of walking with God and choosing not to take the burden back onto my shoulders. It was years of continuing to trust Him by putting one foot in front of the other, one day after another.

Yes, everything changed that first night—because I abandoned the burden instead of continuing to carry it.

One of my all-time favourite movies is *Forrest Gump*. There's a scene where Forrest is a little boy and has braces on his legs. He can barely walk. One day, some really mean boys come by and start throwing rocks at him, and he has no choice but to try running away. As he begins to run, he experiences a miracle. The braces break apart and Forrest begins to run free for the first time in his life.

When I saw this scene for the very first time, it touched me deeply. I not only saw Forrest, I saw myself. Even though I didn't have physical braces on my legs, I had invisible braces all over my life. These braces said, "You're not good enough, Sam! No one's ever gonna love you. You've got no future. You've got no family and you might as well kill yourself, and the sooner the better!"

But on the most hopeless night of my life, God broke those braces free. He took me by the hand and began to lead me out of the darkness.

Right now, I want you to think about your life. Ask yourself this question: in the brief time you have left on this planet, what might God want to do in your life that will facilitate more freedom than you've ever experienced before?

I absolutely love that one scene in *Forrest Gump*, but the best part comes a bit later as he runs across a beautiful green field. That beautiful field represents two specific experiences in my life. One was when God began to free me from my invisible braces as a teenager.

The second experience is more recent, more fresh and painful—and it concerns my marriage.

My wife Rita and I have gone through seasons in our marriage where both of us have been bound up, entrenched in our corners and out of sorts with each other and ourselves. At these times, we've hurt each other and our relationship, not knowing how to stop the downwards spiral. If it had been easy to leave each other, we might have been tempted to walk away. In fact, we *were* tempted to walk away. We knew deep down that God wasn't calling us to that, though. So we surrendered ourselves and our marriage to God and each other in a fresh and vulnerable way.

Now, I'm not judging anyone who has a failed marriage, because it takes two people to make it work—two people who will give themselves to God and each other even when it doesn't make sense, even when it doesn't feel right, even when it seems as though there's no hope whatsoever.

Even in our worst moments as husband and wife, we were on the edge of incredible. But it sure didn't feel like it at the time.

Nine

HOLY HEZEKIAH BATMAN

Hezekiah was a king in the southern territory of Judah around seven hundred years before the time of Jesus. He was a good man, a godly king who sought the Lord. Hezekiah did things right. However, the neighbouring king of Assyria was invading countries all around the region.

Some things haven't changed that much.

Assyria had way more men, way more strength, and way more political power. On paper, Hezekiah had no hope and no future. But the prophet Isaiah came to Hezekiah one day and shared this message: *"[The Lord] will be the sure foundation for your times, a rich store of salvation and wisdom and knowledge; the fear of the Lord is the key to this treasure"* (Isaiah 33:6, NIV).

We won't get into it here, but I've done my research on this scripture—the time they were living in, who this man was, who his enemies were, and what was happening. I firmly believe God is giving us this truth so that we can also apply it to our lives today.

King Hezekiah felt overwhelmed. He couldn't change his outward circumstances. Here he was, completely swamped with trouble, and God sent someone to him to say, "Don't give up. You're on the edge of incredible here."

Today, God has sent me to give you the very same message: "Don't you dare give up! You are on the edge of incredible here!" I know it doesn't feel like it, but you don't have to believe every feeling you have today.

And here's why. The Lord says that He *will be your sure foundation, providing a rich store of salvation, wisdom, and knowledge. The fear of the Lord will be your treasure.*

Now, the fear of the Lord we're speaking about here doesn't refer to terror. It's not the kind of fear a person might have if they woke up and found a five-foot snake in their bed.

The fear of the Lord we're talking about is a reverence, respect, and holy awe that leads to obedience. In other words, we have enough of an understanding of how incredible God is that we are filled with awe of who He is, which leads us to obey Him. We call out to Him, "God, You are God! Help me to follow You. In the ways my heart doesn't want to follow You, change my heart."

If you choose to fear the Lord, you don't have to be afraid of anybody or anything, including suffering or death, because He will make a way for you.

Did you know that there are more verses in the Bible speaking against fear than any other topic? "Do not be afraid." I think I'm on safe theological ground when I tell you that the Lord wants you to bring your fear and leave it with Him.

Right in this moment, will you choose to lay down your fears and anxieties to God, or will you continue with your invisible but very real backpack of fear-filled emotional baggage?

I encourage you to take this question seriously, realizing that if you don't make an active choice to lay down the backpack, you're actually choosing to tighten the straps. Avoiding the question is simply another way to double down on your own slavery.

It was gifted pastor, counsellor, and songwriter Jack Hayford who posed this thought well worth considering: "How would you treat a friend who lies to you as much as fear has?"[6]

In the past, I've given fear way too much authority over my life. But by God's grace, my fear is shrinking and my faith is expanding exponentially.

Romans 8:15 puts it this way: *"So you have not received a spirit that makes you fearful slaves. Instead, you received God's Spirit when he adopted you as his own children. Now we call him, 'Abba, Father.'"*

If you've chosen to follow Jesus, if you've received His forgiveness for your sins, you are in the family. It's not about what you do to achieve standing in the family. You are in the family, completely. You can receive the benefit of the fact that the living God is your Father.

But change will only happen in your life when one of two things take place: when your level of discomfort becomes greater than your level of fear, or when your awareness of being loved and accepted becomes greater than your awareness of fear.

Either we need to be so uncomfortable that it overcomes our fear or we need to realize how incredibly loved we are. And when that comes over us like a wave, it will override the fear. Those are the two doorways that lead to real change.

---

6 "Jack Hayford," *Daily Christian Quote.* November 5, 2011 (https://www.dailychristianquote.com/jack-hayford-2/).

Ten
BRAKE FLUID FLUSH

Do you know what a brake fluid flush is? Proudly raise your hand if you do, even if you're reading on a crowded bus!

Basically, a car has brakes on the wheel and a brake pedal inside. In between, there are tubes (brake lines) filled with brake fluid. I'm no mechanic, so this is simplified, but when you step on the brake pedal, it exerts force on the fluid, which puts pressure on the actual brakes.

Over time, and after travelling a hundred thousand kilometres or so, the brake fluid starts to break down. It gets dirty and actually begins to damage the whole braking system because the fluid is no longer pure.

That's when the mechanics recommend doing a brake fluid flush. They inject clean fluid into the brake lines at one end and pump the fluid through the whole system. Guess what shoots out the other end? The dirty, broken-down brake fluid that has been doing damage to the system. They keep pumping the clean stuff in until all the dirty stuff has been forced out. When the clean fluid starts coming out the other end, they know they have eliminated the dirty fluid from the system.

You know, I'm a little weird. I get that. You wouldn't be the first one to tell me so. But when I recently read in the Bible that perfect love drives out fear, I thought about a brake fluid flush.

From time to time, I need a "fear flush" in my own heart and life. I need God's perfect love to drive out the fear. It can creep in subtly and silently, like ants who find spilled honey on the kitchen floor.

The fear attaches itself to us in thousands of different ways. We compare the best of what we see in others to the worst of what we see in ourselves. We tell ourselves that we could have been happy and living without fear "if only things had been different." We promise ourselves that we will stop letting fear control us "one day."

I remember that first "one day" in my own life. I was six years old and our first-grade class had joined the second-graders to watch a movie one afternoon. Wow, those second-graders really looked like they had it all together! Not insecure and scared and clueless like I felt. I thought to myself that life would really begin once I got to Grade Two!

But then I got to Grade Two and felt just like I had in Grade One, except we didn't get to take an afternoon nap on our little mats on the classroom floor anymore.

Grade Two is small potatoes, I thought to myself. *Grade Seven is where the action is. You get to be king of the elementary school!*

So I waited five more years until I was twelve years old and in Grade Seven. Yet somehow I still felt similar to my Grade One self, only taller and with the promise of impending pimples.

I then theorized that life would really begin when I was thirteen. I'd be bold and unafraid in junior high. Oops. Nope. High school? Nada. College? You guessed it.

I finally realized that life wasn't going to start once some outside occurrence was achieved, but only once a transformational occurrence happened *inside* me. I needed a fear flush, and thank God that He gave me one![7]

These days, I regularly hook up my heart to two specific scriptures. The first is found in the Old Testament, and the second is from the New Testament. As I deeply receive the fullness of the power contained in these words from God, the fear can't help but get squeezed out and rendered impotent.

The Lord sent a prophet named Isaiah to speak on His behalf to the people He loves, including you and me. In Isaiah 43:1, he says, *"[L]isten to the Lord who created you… the one who formed you says, 'Do not be afraid, for I have ransomed you. I have called you by name; you are mine.'"*

Now, don't just brush by this. If this is true, it changes everything! The living God, the creator of this universe and everything in it, is telling you that He has paid the price required for your freedom! You are no longer a prisoner trapped by shackles of fear. He has called you by your name and you belong to Him.

At this moment, you are very much like one of the Mauritian ex-slaves up on the mountaintop.

Your very next step is the most important one you'll ever take. Will it be a step of fear, a turning away from hope and life, like those of the precious but fear-soaked Mauritians on that fateful day? Or will it be a glorious step of faith into the Father's arms as you choose to believe that you've been made free and that God Himself paid the bill?

---

[7] You'll hear more about that when I tell you the swimming pool story a little later in the book.

It gets even better. I would love for you to be able to receive this next scripture as fully and completely as possible, so I invite you to prepare your heart and mind in a few simple ways.

Take a few slow deep breaths and put any tension or anxiety you may have on the back burner for a few minutes. Now, imagine yourself in a favourite place in the great outdoors. You might imagine yourself sitting by the ocean or walking in the forest or perhaps sitting by a campfire.

Are you able to make a little room in your heart for what you're about to hear? I hope so, because you'll find it is well worth making room for.

As you see yourself in your mind's eye, in your beautiful spot in nature, imagine that Jesus comes and sits down beside you. He smiles at you in a way that makes your soul light up. And then He says to you, "I have chosen you."

You have not chosen Me, but I have chosen you and I have appointed and placed and purposefully planted you, so that you would go and bear fruit and keep on bearing, and that your fruit will remain and be lasting, so that whatever you ask of the Father in My name [as My representative] He may give to you. This [is what] I command you: that you love and unselfishly seek the best for one another. (John 15:16–17, AMP)

Now, that sounds like a life worth living. Responding to Jesus's call on your life by taking a big, beautiful step of faith is what you were born for.

Jesus, flush the fear out of our lives so that we can live this new life of faith with You, starting right now.

Eleven
WHAT'S IN YOUR CHECKING ACCOUNT?

I've spent too much of my time having private individual bank accounts with the people in my life. If they do good things and make me happy, it's a deposit. If they disappoint me or hurt me, it's a withdrawal. I then interact with them based on their current account balance.

There have been times when I felt like I had several accounts in either very poor shape or completely overdrawn!

Sounds kind of reasonable. I thought so, too, until I realized I can live out of the unlimited balance God has given me in my account with Him. To put it another way, I don't need to interact with people based on what I feel they've deposited in our relational account. Instead, I can interact with people based on the unlimited relational resources God has deposited into my life.

Now, this doesn't mean I let people take advantage of me or abuse me, just because God has invested so much in me. But it does mean I can set appropriate boundaries with unsafe or untrustworthy people while still living graciously, generously, and joyfully. None of it is dependent on how much is in each individual relational bank account.

Even if I have only ten dollars in my jeans, I can still give it away as I walk down the street, because I know that I have a lot more in my actual, physical bank account. Even though that other person has not invested in me, I'm free to give because I've been blessed with much, much more.

In the same way, we can afford to give more than we get to those in our lives because God has poured so much more over us. We have extra to spare!

We don't have to size up every relationship to make sure that things are fair. That's exhausting! Instead, we can live with great freedom as we invest in those around us without keeping score.

Twelve

I COULD REALLY BE FREE IF...

I had been invited to speak to a group of 250 people who were meeting for a weeklong event. Because we were spending some extended time together, I had the opportunity to go deeper with them than I might have been able to in the course of just one or two talks.

I decided to conduct a bit of an experiment with them. Now we have the opportunity to benefit from their honesty and courage.

On the third day of our event, I handed out a three-by-five inch card that said, "Dear God, I could really be free if…" I asked them to anonymously complete the card with as much honesty and transparency as they could.

I was moved by their responses.

Of the hundreds of cards that came back with personal responses, the replies were amazingly unified into two distinct themes, demonstrating the two biggest things that hold us back from really living. See if you resonate with these responses.

Issue One: Unforgiveness

- Dear God, I could really be free if… I could easily forgive people and not hold onto the hurts.
- Dear God, I could really be free if… I could be more forgiving and have some semblance of happiness.
- Dear God, I could really be free if… I let go of resentment/ bitterness, as I use it to feel superior over those who have hurt me.
- Dear God, I could really be free if… I let go of my past mistakes and guilt. If I could truly forgive…

Issue Two: Worry About How Others Perceive Me

- Dear God, I could really be free if… I didn't care what other people thought of me.
- Dear God, I could really be free if… I could stop seeking the approval of other people.
- Dear God, I could really be free if… I didn't worry about what people thought of me.
- Dear God, I could really be free if… I could let go of my need for the approval of other people. I am so concerned with myself.

When I think about what has weighed me down from living fully, these are also my top two issues.

It's the last sentence of the last card that really holds the key, though: "I am so concerned with myself." If we make ourselves the centre of our universe and attempt to have everything revolve around ourselves, peace will continue to be elusive.

Honestly, this is where I start to get really excited and hopeful. Because these issues aren't only important to you and me but to God. So important, in fact, that He paid an unimaginable price to address them and free us from their grip.

Let's examine something radical that Jesus invited us to do. In Matthew 10:39, He says, *"If your first concern is to look after yourself, you'll never find yourself. But if you forget about yourself and look to me, you'll find both yourself and me"* (MSG).

How many joyful, self-centred people do you know, people whose first concern is themselves? Take your time.

Funny thing, I don't know any either. I also know that, ironically, I've been the most unhappy when I'm most consumed with myself and my happiness.

Why should we give weight to Jesus's invitation to forget about ourselves and look to Him? Well, He said this about Himself: *"If you really knew me, you would know my Father as well. From now on, you do know him. You've even seen him!"* (John 14:7, MSG)

Jesus is saying here that when you know Him, you know God. And when you've seen Him, you've seen God. That's not something a "good teacher" or a "great man of morals" would say. C.S. Lewis pointed out that Jesus is either the Son of the living God, or a liar, or a crazy man.[8] Each one of us has to decide for ourselves which of these three Jesus is.

I'm betting my life that Jesus is God's only Son, because many years ago I let go of my own life to embrace His life, and He changed everything for me.

But back to our two issues: unforgiveness and trying to be people-pleasers.

This idea of letting go of ourselves to embrace Jesus is closely tied to finding real freedom in forgiveness and being okay with the idea that we can't please everyone.

---

[8] C.S. Lewis, *Mere Christianity* (New York, NY: Macmillian/Collier, 1952), 55.

Perhaps if we find deep and full forgiveness from the living God of the universe, we will be suddenly empowered to let the chains of bitterness and unforgiveness slip off our hearts and minds.

And when we allow our souls to receive the unconditional acceptance of the living God of the universe, we can make peace with life, even if we don't experience the conditional acceptance of every person in our relational web. After all, Jesus Himself wasn't accepted by everyone in His world—or our world, for that matter. What kind of twisted mentality would demand that you or I achieve that?

I've found that when my first concern is to look after myself and put me on the throne of my own life, I get very focussed on all the wrongs that have been done to me and all the people who should like me or love me more than I feel they do.

But if I begin to forget about myself and look to Jesus, I discover that He has forgiven me at the immeasurable cost of His own life on the cross. Suddenly I'm not keeping score of everyone else's sins and what they owe me anymore. It's actually very freeing to realize that nobody owes me anything, because Jesus has already given me everything I need for life and for living with freedom.

I realize that I can forgive others in the rising tide of God's forgiveness for me, but at some point, I have to face an even tougher issue: forgiving myself.

We can be so hard on ourselves. Holocaust survivor Dr. Edith Eger said that she was able to forgive Hitler and the commanding officer at Auschwitz, but it took her decades to forgive herself for not being able to save her own mother's life at that Nazi death camp.[9] Would you expect a teenaged girl to

---

[9] Eger, *The Choice*, 231–232.

be able to save her mother from the deadly power of the Third Reich? Of course not.

In the Lord's Prayer, Jesus invites us to pray, *"[F]orgive us our sins, as we forgive those who sin against us"* (Luke 11:4). It's clear that we are not to continue holding ourselves captive to what we ask the Lord to release us from. That would make no sense at all.

So where do we need to apply grace and forgiveness to our own hearts and lives today?

The forgiveness of Jesus is so powerful that there's not one human being who isn't forgivable. Even as Jesus was being murdered on the cross, He was asking His Father in heaven for these killers to be forgiven. If Jesus is willing to forgive the people who murdered Him, He is more than willing to forgive you, even for the darkest and most horrific and shameful of sins. Jesus is all about bringing freedom and forgiveness to the deepest parts of your soul.

It's not the size of your sin that counts, but the size of your Saviour! Nothing brings more glory to God than the forgiven and free children of God who have learned to dance with joy in the acceptance and grace that their Father in heaven is pouring over them. It brings no joy to God if we choose to remain stuck in unforgiveness for ourselves and others.

And why do we have the goal and expectation that everyone should love us, celebrate us, and continually think well of us? Perhaps if we accepted ourselves as we are and experienced the intimate friendship of God daily, we wouldn't need to depend on everyone else to prop up our self-esteem.

I'm not talking about having a big ego and being self-centred. I'm talking about being realistic about our strengths and weaknesses. Knowing that we are loved and valued by our creator empowers us to love and value ourselves, even if some other people choose not to love and value us.

Italian author and playwright Luigi Pirandello, winner of the 1934 Nobel Prize for Literature, communicated an amazing and mind-expanding concept in his book, *One, No One & 100,000*. Basically, he writes that a different version of you exists in the minds of everyone who has ever met you, even those who have just seen you on the street. You aren't the "one person" you think of yourself as being in your own mind. Your spouse sees you as one person, while your brother has a different view of you. Your neighbour has yet an additional view of who you are, and so on. Perhaps there are thousands of versions of you in thousands of people's minds.

If we take this idea to heart, we'll realize that attempting to unify everyone's concept of ourselves into one that is one hundred percent positive, appreciated, and adored is one hundred percent *impossible*. Having this goal is your free ticket to increased anxiety and devalued self-worth.

Of the thousands of versions of "me" that are out there in different people's minds, I choose to focus on the version that is held gently and firmly in the mind and heart of my creator.

Ephesians 2:10 says, *"For we are God's masterpiece. He has created us anew in Christ Jesus, so we can do the good things he planned for us long ago."* That's my picture of us: God's masterpieces—not because we're so amazing, but because He is, and we are His creation. I think that's a version of ourselves worth considering.

On top of this, consider what's written in Psalm 139:17: *"How precious are your thoughts about me, O God. They cannot be numbered! I can't even count them; they outnumber the grains of sand! And when I wake up, you are still with me!"*

You are deeply valued by the one who made the countless billions and billions of stars in our universe—more stars than there are grains of sand on the earth! He thinks of you more than He thinks of all of them. It's not because of what you have done. It's because of who you belong to.

And now, because of who you belong to, you're free to forget about yourself as you fall in love with your Father in heaven for the very first time, or for the ten-thousandth time. His forgiveness and grace and love and life are in the process of flooding your soul in such a fresh and powerful way that your (super)natural response to those around you will be to pour forgiveness, grace, love, and life over them. It won't be something you *have* to do; it will be something you *can't stop* from being done through you.

> It is absolutely clear that God has called you to a free life. Just make sure that you don't use this freedom as an excuse to do whatever you want to do and destroy your freedom. Rather, use your freedom to serve one another in love; that's how freedom grows. For everything we know about God's Word is summed up in a single sentence: Love others as you love yourself. That's an act of true freedom. (Galatians 5:13–14, MSG)

Thirteen

MY HELICOPTER RIDE

I once had the incredible opportunity to fly in a helicopter around Whistler and Blackcomb Mountains, two of the most beautiful skiing areas in the whole world. Better yet, I was given the front seat in the cockpit, right beside the pilot.

Because the helicopter had a transparent plastic bubble around its front end, the view exceeded my highest expectations. I could look above me, around me, and below me almost at the same time. Phenomenal!

I was only inches away from the pilot, able to see all the helicopter's controls, though I certainly didn't understand what they all meant. I saw a rather large gauge that fluctuated between 97 and 105 kilometres per hour. I was really surprised by that.

"Wow," I said to the pilot. "It's amazing that we're going around 100 kilometres per hour."

He replied nonchalantly, "We're going 65 kilometres per hour."

"Oh. Am I reading that gauge wrong, the one that says 99 kilometres per hour?"

"Nope." Then he just sat there quietly.

Hmm, you should really get that fixed, I thought.

But it was as if the pilot read my mind. "It's not broken, Sam. It's working fine."

Okay, I'd had enough of this game and wanted to clear a few things up. "Mr. Pilot, are you telling me that the gauge that says we've been going 99 kilometres per hour isn't broken, but that we are in fact going 65 kilometres per hour?"

"Yup."

"Well, what am I missing here, sir?" I figured upping the respect factor might help move things along a little bit.

"The gauge you've been reading is the airspeed indicator. That's the speed at which the air is coming into contact with the front of the helicopter. The air *is* contacting the front of the helicopter at 99 kilometres per hour, but we have a headwind of approximately 34 kilometres per hour. Thus, our true airspeed is 65 kilometres per hour."

"And how do you determine that?"

"Do you see this gauge that says 65?" he asked politely.

"Yup," I said, doing my best impersonation of the pilot. He picked up on my teasing tone and we both chuckled a bit.

"Well, that gauge gets information from three different satellites simultaneously. By triangulating the information from those satellites, it's able to determine our true airspeed."

For the next twenty minutes, we floated effortlessly over the beautiful mountains and valleys around Whistler. All the while, I thought about what this pilot and his helicopter were teaching me.

Do you realize that you and I have an airspeed indicator, too? It's called our emotions. We can feel very strongly that we're going in a certain direction at a certain speed, but like the helicopter, we need to get additional information from three different satellites so we can tell with accuracy where we're going and how fast we're travelling.

As I write these words today, it's May 2020. We're in the middle of a worldwide lockdown due to the COVID-19 pandemic. My feelings have been telling me that I'm going nowhere fast. It could get really depressing, too. It feels like I'm being quite unproductive.

Fortunately, I'm getting my real data from three sources today: the word of God, the Spirit of God, and people in my life who are full of wisdom and maturity.

For example, I read in the word of God today, *"The Lord will fulfill his purpose for me"* (Psalm 138:8, ESV). Wow! That's such great news. So it's not up to me to figure everything out? Hallelujah! The Lord will do it. I just need to make myself available for His purposes.

As I draw near to the Spirit of God, He confirms what the word of God says: "You are accepted. You are forgiven. I am with you!"

More great news.

When I talk with a wise brother in the Lord, he tells me that the Lord is at work in our lives and that we should step out in faith and trust Him for it. Suddenly my feelings of uselessness, of spinning my wheels, are overtaken by the Lord, who triangulates the proverbial satellites in my life to give me a whole new perspective on where I'm going!

Yes, during this season of COVID-19 I can't travel and speak to groups of young people around the world and share my hope in Jesus with them. But it was never about what I was doing in the first place. It was always about Him and what He is doing.

In fact, Romans 12:3 puts it this way: *"The only accurate way to understand ourselves is by what God is and by what he does for us, not by what we are and what we do for him"* (MSG). That's a perfect example of how these satellites can give us a more accurate understanding of the truth.

God's got this, and He will make a way in His time.

He's also got you. Even if your airspeed indicator, your feelings, are going a little crazy at the moment, remember that God's word, God's Spirit, and a few mature and wise friends can help you to get where you were meant to go and arrive at just the right time.

Fourteen
THE ROCK THAT SHATTERED YOUR STAINED-GLASS WINDOW

In Philip Yancey's great book *Reaching for the Invisible God,* he tells a brief (and true) story of a particular stained-glass window in Winchester Cathedral.[10] The cathedral itself is located in Hampshire, England, and during the civil war of 1642 Oliver Cromwell's men entered the church and proceeded to smash one of the most beautiful windows. Their goal was to destroy the hopes and dreams of the people there, and in that, they almost succeeded.

Back in those days, many people could neither read nor write, so the pictures in the stained-glass told them the Bible's stories of love and light in a way they could understand. I can only imagine how heavy their hearts became as the bricks flew through that window, smashing the carefully placed panes of coloured glass and sending them crashing to the ground.

The people had three possible responses to this heartbreaking situation, and I imagine that some responded in each of these ways.

---

[10] Philip Yancey, *Reaching for the Invisible God* (Grand Rapids, MI: Zondervan, 2000), 277.

Firstly, some would have picked up the broken glass in their hands and cried out, "Look what they have done to us!" Grief-stricken and overwhelmed with anguish, they probably wouldn't have noticed that their own hands were being cut by the shards of glass as they were squeezed in a passionate grip.

Most likely there was a second group who, while hurting just as deeply, responded by neither picking up the broken shards nor crying out about their fate. They carried on with their day-to-day lives, albeit with a newfound sombreness. They still went to work each day and attended Sunday services at church, but they lost all hope in hope itself.

There was a third group, however. We know for certain this group existed because of what eventually became of the broken pieces of glass. This group may have been tempted to react like those in the first or second groups, and perhaps for a time they did, but eventually they chose an entirely different response. Because they had a deep relationship with their creator, they cried out to God, a small flicker of hope still burning in their souls. They said to the Lord, "Father, You are the creator. The stained-glass window has been shattered. It's not at all how we wanted it to be, but we believe You can take these broken shards of colour and make something new with them, make something even more beautiful than what we had before."

Psalm 143:8 says, *"Show me your faithful love this morning. I trust in you. Show me what I should do. I put my life in your hands!"* (ERV)

Just like the believers at Winchester Cathedral, we need to experience God's faithful love so that we will be encouraged to trust Him and do what He asks us to do.

So this third group asked God to take the broken pieces of their stained-glass window and empower their minds and hands so they could, in partnership with the Lord, make something new and beautiful together.

Shockingly, the people had to store the broken pieces for eighteen years, until the political situation made it possible for them to rebuild the windows into a brand-new pattern. After this long, long wait, they began placing the broken pieces in new and unexpected patterns, and once the window was rebuilt it became more famous and adored than even the original window. It was, in fact, modern art centuries ahead of its time.

I'm betting you once had a perfect picture of what you wanted your life to be. I'm also betting that somewhere along the line, a relationship or situation threw a brick into your ideal life, right through the middle of your stained-glass window. And today, just like the people of another time at Westminster Cathedral, you're facing a huge pile of sharp and broken pieces of what used to be your ideal life.

Unfortunately, recreating the original dream isn't an option. Going back in time and stopping the destruction also isn't possible. There is just you and the broken pieces.

But that doesn't mean you are powerless. In fact, just the opposite is true. While you can't change what has happened, you can decide how you will respond and if you will move forward or backward. It has been said that you can't go back and change the beginning of your story, but you can start where you are and change the ending.

Earlier in this book, I mentioned Dr. Edith Eger, author of *The Choice*. Even though she went through some of the most horrific events any human being could endure, she never asked,

"Why me?" Instead she quietly whispered to herself, "What's next?" This kept her moving forward.

We can choose to be like some of the Westminster Cathedral congregation, who picked up the broken glass and screamed, "Look what they did to me!" Or we can be like those who quietly lost hope and allowed the light to dim from their eyes and the fire to die in their hearts.

There is a third option, though. We can draw near to the Lord and say, "Father, You are the author of creation and creativity. Would You take these jagged and broken pieces of my life? Make something beautiful with them, even though this isn't at all what I expected or intended for my life."

For some of us, the smashed stained-glass window is our family of origin. For others, it is our marriage. For yet others, it is our job situation or health.

We can spend the rest of our lives screaming, "Look what they did to me!" We can become sombre and hopeless. Or we can say to the Lord, "What's next, Father? What can I learn from this? How will You choose to reshape my heart so that I can receive my own healing and become an agent of healing and hope in the lives of others? Father in heaven, make something beautiful out of the broken pieces of my life."

It takes faith to invite the Lord to transform your wound into a scar and your pain into a memory that, while never forgotten, no longer controls your thoughts and emotions. Your broken stained-glass window doesn't need to control the trajectory of your life any longer.

Instead of pulling your heart and your spirit towards heaviness and despair, be reinvigorated with hope as you experience your creator recreating you. He will patiently lead you to a place of new life and colour and light, beyond the brokenness and jagged, cutting edges you have experienced in the past.

How do I know this for sure? Because I am living proof. And I'm reaching out to you right now, inviting you to take the hand of God. He created a beautiful world in the beginning, and you will be amazed by what He'll recreate in your life.

Writer and speaker Robin Sharma says, "All change is hard at first, messy in the middle and so gorgeous at the end."[11] The real miracle is that Jesus unselfishly entered into that hard and messy work on our behalf, before we ever knew or even cared about Him.

Having laid down His own life for us, Jesus gently invites us to join Him in our mess, where He has patiently waited for us, so that together we can finally start living in freedom, forgiveness, and beauty.

[11] Robin Sharma, "All change is hard at first ..." *Twitter*. April 8, 2014 (https://twitter.com/robinsharma/status/453472361421877248?lang=en).

Fifteen
THIRTY YEARS A SLAVE

With the unconditional surrender of the Empire of Japan on September 2, 1945, World War Two finally came to an end in the South Pacific.

Lieutenant Hiroo Onoda was a passionate young Japanese soldier who had been stationed on a remote island in the Philippines in 1944. His mission had been to conduct guerrilla warfare and gather intelligence. Unfortunately, no one bothered to inform him when the war ended a year later!

After some time, leaflets were dropped into the jungle to communicate with him and let him know that peace had come. He was no longer a pawn, forced to hide. He had the opportunity to live in freedom, to return home, to start a family, to follow his dreams.

Regrettably, he didn't believe the good news.

Onoda was so entrenched in his way of thinking that he couldn't see any other options for his life. What a waste, to spend an extra year or two at war, including with yourself, especially when the war no longer exists. It would be an even greater waste to spend five or ten years fighting a battle that only lives on in your mind.

But Onoda didn't just waste one or two years, or even five or ten. In fact, he stayed hidden in the jungle, at war with himself and the world around him, for almost thirty more years! He finally claimed his freedom on March 10, 1975.

He had been twenty-one years old when he was placed on that little island, and he was fifty-two years old when he left. Not only did he waste twenty-nine years of his life there unnecessarily, he also injured and even killed many inhabitants of the island whom he incorrectly believed to be his enemies. Freedom, hope, and a future were all available to him, but for more than half his life he either didn't know it or wouldn't believe it.

Fortunately for him, after almost three decades he finally came out of the jungle and found his freedom. He began to experience the incredible life that had been waiting so patiently to be discovered.

In Luke 4:18–19, Jesus quotes the prophet Isaiah and declares His mission to impact the world and change the trajectory of your journey, His incredible mission to declare peace over you and your life:

The Spirit of the Lord is upon me, for he has anointed me to bring Good News to the poor. He has sent me to proclaim that captives will be released, that the blind will see, that the oppressed will be set free, and that the time of the Lord's favor has come.

Jesus wants to pour the Lord's favour out over your life. Are you ready to receive what He has been patiently waiting to give to you, or do you prefer to remain on an island of your own making?

Sixteen
FREE TICKETS TO THE THEATRE OF MY MIND

Yesterday I unexpectedly saw an ultra-high-definition video play across the theatre of my mind. I hadn't been anticipating it and I certainly didn't consciously choose to start playing it. It was more like the sudden popups that sometimes appear on a website.

Just before it started to play, I had been thinking about how knowledge is a good thing, but that a revelation from God can change everything.

Merriam-Webster defines revelation as "an act of revealing or communicating divine truth."[12] I can study the Bible for years and increase my knowledge, but from time to time I need a revelation download.

So these were my thoughts at the time, though I didn't know they were to become the opening credits for my mind's latest cinematic release.

In the scene, I stood five feet behind myself, watching anonymously. I could see my shirtless back, and shockingly

---

[12] "Revelation," *Merriam-Webster*. Date of access: August 9, 2020 (https://www.merriam-webster.com/dictionary/revelation)

I noticed two fishhooks piercing my flesh, one over my right shoulder blade and another just left of centre, about six inches lower. The hooks had gone through my skin cleanly enough, but removing them would be too agonizing an option to even consider. Each hook still had a slender nylon fishing line attached, though I couldn't see where the lines led.

I became aware that Jesus was there, standing just behind me.

"Do you want to get rid of these?" He asked.

Though He didn't explain it to me, I instinctively knew what these fishhooks were—past hurts and frustrations I was holding against others. I also knew that the other end of the fishing lines were held by the evil one, and that he delighted in yanking on the lines to watch me squirm.

As long as these barbs remained in my back, someone else had control over me.

I nodded to Jesus, and He set to work. First He used wire cutters to clip the barbs off the end of the hooks. Then He backed the curved wire remnants out of the wounds. He repeated the procedure with the second hook.

I was surprised by the ease with which they were removed.

Then, as quickly and unexpectedly as the mental movie had started, it was over.

I've been pondering these images ever since, and today I stumbled across Psalm 111:2, which says, *"How amazing are the deeds of the Lord! All who delight in him should ponder them."*

Once again I find myself thinking about how knowledge is a good thing, but that a revelation from God can change everything. Because of God's great works, I no longer need to fight through this life like a fish on the end of a hook, and neither do you.

Seventeen
MY FATHER-IN-LAW'S GIFT

I'm not proud of the story you're about to hear, and I'm okay if you think less of me after finding this out. The potential of your enhanced freedom is more important than my reputation.

It was Easter dinner 2008, and my family and I were at my in-laws' for a wonderful meal that Farm Oma, my wife Rita's mom, had worked very hard to prepare.

Trouble had been brewing between one of my young adult children and myself for at least a year—and it wasn't just any of my children; it was the one who most reminds me of… me.

Somehow as dinner progressed, statements were made from both sides of the table that inflamed the situation. Before I realized it, I lost control of my temper and the "discussion" escalated into a loud and insensitive argument.

While my child didn't handle things overly well, I was supposed to have been the mature one, the one setting a good example. That day, I failed miserably. It's not an understatement to say that I had singlehandedly ruined what was supposed to have been a celebratory dinner of thankfulness, faith, and family.

We all drove home from Oma and Opa's in stone silence. My embarrassment and self-humiliation were almost unbearable. How could I have blown it this badly? My wife was embarrassed and ashamed of me, and rightly so. My emotional and verbal explosion had created relational shrapnel that injured every single person in our beautiful family.

That night as I lay in bed unable to sleep, I rolled the scenario over and over in my mind. Where had I gone off the rails? How could I stop this from ever happening again? Would I ever be able to repair the relational damage I had so exuberantly dished out at the dinner table? How could I have spoken this way to the most important people in my life?

I decided at 4:24 in the morning that at first light I would drive over to my in-laws' house and beg for their forgiveness. I thought it quite likely they would throw me out, or perhaps not even let me through their door in the first place, but I had to try.

As I made the thirty-minute drive to their farmhouse, it seemed as though every negative scenario played on a never-ending loop in my mind. I almost turned back several times as the dark grey clouds of hopelessness stormed over my heart.

When I arrived, I didn't dare park in my usual spot in the driveway, close to their front door. Instead, I parked much farther down the street, out of view. I didn't want them to know I was there until the moment I knocked on the door, the same one I always used to enter without knocking at all.

As I walked towards the house, I thought about all the special times I'd had with these people, who in a very real sense had become a mother and father to me. Had I damaged our relationship beyond repair?

My heart pounded as I knocked on the old farmhouse door. Opa soon appeared and opened it, saying nothing at all. He motioned for me to come in.

Being a man of few words at the best of times, it was impossible to read his body language during the painful silence as we walked to the living room. He motioned again, this time for me to take a seat. Surprisingly, Oma was already sitting there, as if she had been patiently waiting the whole time.

"I don't even know where to start," I began as tears made their way down my face. "I've been struggling with my anger and emotions for some time and I've promised Rita that I'm going to get help. I'm so very sorry for how I behaved last night. I will understand if you can't forgive me, but I'm asking if you might consider trying to. I'm making an appointment with a counsellor to help me deal with my inner frustrations and turmoil, and I'm going to see another couple to pray over me and do you think you could ever forgive me and…"

Opa cut me off mid-sentence with a completely unexpected question: "Sam, where is your car?"

"Well, I parked it down the street in case you didn't want to have anything to do with me. I assumed you might not want me to park on your property."

And then the man of few words poured life over me.

"Sam," he said. "You are part of this family. You always will be. There is nothing you can do to change that. You can never *not* be part of this family."

Those dark grey storm clouds of hopelessness started to crack open as some unexpected sunlight poured around their jagged edges.

Never on this earth have I experienced a scenario that has taught me more about God's heart towards His children, towards me, and towards you. Haven't we all blown it and wondered if our Father in heaven has given up on us? I know I have, and more than once or twice.

Yet my father-in-law unknowingly modelled the incredible, undeserved grace and acceptance of our Father in heaven when He said, "You are part of this family. You can never *not* be part of this family."

This is the very core of God's heart towards you. He wants you to be part of His family—not parking down the street, not even knocking on the door. He just wants you to swing it wide open as you come in, to begin being loved and loving in return.

But if you need to, park your car down the street this one last time. Knock on the door if you don't feel comfortable walking in just yet. But come. Your heart may be pounding now, but you'll be accepted just like I was that day.

I have a unique and wonderful father-in-law and his actions that day will always reflect our unique and wonderful Father-of-grace.

P.S. I also met with my adult daughter and asked for her forgiveness for the poor example I set that night at dinner. She was equally gracious to me.

Eighteen
REALLY LIVING OR JUST NOT DYING?

It's 12:25 a.m. and I'm flying somewhere over northern Africa. Algeria maybe? I head to the washroom at the back of the plane, and while I'm there I check my front pocket to make sure I haven't misplaced my passport.

It's very dark in the cabin of the plane, but in the washroom I pull out the passport and look at it. It's so beat up. Almost every page has a stamp or sticker from one country or another. It's so worn that it's starting to fall apart.

Then I look up and see my face in the mirror. I can't help but notice the similarities. There are deep lines in my face from hundreds of thousands of individual smiles, and more than a few tears as well. My skin is weathered and worn from facing the new day more than twenty thousand times now.

Why do we yearn to look untarnished and perfect? As I look at my passport, I remember real adventures and amazing experiences with incredible souls.

Perhaps instead of being ashamed of our faces, we should wear them proudly. We have lived. We have experienced gut-wrenching heartache, but we have also loved deeply. We have made mistakes, even hurt people, but we have sought forgiveness and received it as well.

I'm kind of proud of my old beat-up passport. It represents life, and so does my weathered face. I'm not a handsome man by the world's standards, but God has given me a face that reminds me that I have lived.

My good friend, music producer Roy Salmond, once told me about Jewish psychotherapist Esther Perel, whose parents were Auschwitz survivors. He quoted Esther's father, who made an insightful observation about his fellow prisoners, set free at the end of World War Two: "There are those that did not die, and there are those that lived."

I'm not satisfied with merely not dying. I hope you want more, too.

Roy went on to say, "Whether we're defeated by hardships or invigorated by them has much to do with our willingness to risk in life again. To risk requires faith, hope, and a fearless freedom for what is to be." I love that.

Jesus said, *"I came that they may have and enjoy life, and have it in abundance [to the full, till it overflows]"* (John 10:10, AMP).

Nineteen
A POD OF KILLER WHALES

In early July last year, I went to the beach with my wife, Rita. It was a perfect summer day, but surprisingly it was about to get even "perfecter".

As we stood with our toes in the sand, looking out at the powerful beauty of the Pacific Ocean, we suddenly saw not one but two pods of killer whales playing in the water. They weren't just swimming, either; they were *actually playing*—breaching and dancing in the rhythm of the waves, oblivious to the crowds that had gathered on the beach to watch them.

As the sun reflected off their beautiful black and white bodies, these magnificent creations brought glory to their creator. They didn't need to do anything; they simply needed to be who they were created to be. It was in their amazing and unpretentious being that they brought such great joy to all who encountered them.

What if you and I trusted God enough to unashamedly be who He made us to be? To love Him and others unashamedly is to dance in His rhythms and let the light of His Son reflect easily and naturally from our lives. How is God leading you today to be true to Him and true to who He made you to be?

That will take you from the edge of incredible right into the very centre of it.

Twenty

CREATING BEAUTY ALONG THE WAY

I'd just arrived at the wild and captivating African savanna that Jacob and Wilma Schoeman call home. The Schoemans had served the Lord and their community on the outskirts of Outjo, Namibia for decades.

Equal parts Paul the Apostle and Indiana Jones, it wasn't unheard of for Jacob to pray for someone one minute and shoot the business end off of a poisonous snake that came too close the next.

"Dear Lord, thank You so much for this beautiful day and these wonderful people. Please help us to *(boom!)* have a blessed time as we serve You together here in our little corner of the world."

Completely unassuming and supremely practical, Jacob is the kind of guy you want on your team as you travel through the African bush. And just as Jacob is a real man's man, so his wife Wilma is the ultimate modern woman. With no electricity or proper lighting in their home, Wilma would get dressed to the nines, readying herself for a big day and then jumping into their four-by-four at five in the morning. Negotiating the often impassable African roads in her simple yet stylish African sandals, Wilma made their SUV do things even its designers could never have imagined.

Both Jacob and Wilma were among the strongest and most capable people my wife and I had ever met. That's partly why Rita and I have been forever impacted by the conversation Wilma was about to have with us.

While drinking coffee just outside their house, we couldn't help but notice the beautiful winding pathway that led from the parking area to the front door. The walkway featured all sorts of beautiful coloured tiles and other unique objects, all placed in intricate and spectacular patterns.

"Wilma," I said, "this pathway is so beautiful!"

Her response reached a very deep part of me: "Several years ago, my son Christian was killed in a motor vehicle accident. He was twenty-five years old. And of course, I was devastated. Even years later, waves of devastation still wash over me from time to time. When the pain becomes too great to bear, I respond by trying to create something beautiful. This pathway has been my response to pain. Each time I feel overwhelmed, I add a new section to the walkway, embedding the cement with special tiles and the broken pieces of coloured glass you noticed today."

Even though the start of something may be painful or disappointing, it can be transformed into something beautiful. As Wilma goes through her life day by day, she creates beauty and reflects the beauty of her creator.

What a powerful concept—responding to pain by creating something beautiful. I thought of how I've responded to pain in the past: lashing out, growing bitter, breaking something, or saying things I could never take back.

Wilma had tapped into something deeply profound.

Over the next weeks and months, I started to experiment with the concept she had shared with us. When I felt lonely and rejected by someone I valued, I used that pain and energy to reach out to someone else, trying to communicate their immense value in my eyes. When I got some bad news in a letter, I wrote a card to encourage someone else and got it out in the post right away. When I was concerned about my finances, I sent a financial gift to help someone in much more dire need than myself.

When the waves of discouragement or disappointment threaten to crash over my head, I now ask myself, *In what way can I create some beauty in this world as a response to the struggle I'm facing today?*

[H]e will give a crown of beauty for ashes, a joyous blessing instead of mourning, festive praise instead of despair. (Isaiah 61:3)

Twenty-One
THE GIFT EXCHANGE

Do you know what a white elephant gift exchange is? Basically, it happens at Christmastime. You take the ugliest piece of junk from your house, like some candle from the seventies your neighbour gave you and which you've always hated—the candle, not the neighbour—and you wrap it up really nice so someone else will take it.

Everyone sits around in a circle with the big pile of nicely wrapped crappuccino in the middle. Then people take turns opening up what they hope will be something amazing. They're all excited, and then, "Shoot! I brought this very same thing last year when I came to this dumb event! I hate this!"

In a white elephant gift exchange, everyone is trying to trade up. They want to get something better. There's always one person who doesn't really know how the game works, so they bring a box of Lindt chocolates or something else really great. And then everyone's trying to trade up to get that box. You count how many people are ahead of you and speculate about how Suzie might go for that particular thing, meaning you'll have to play the game a certain way to get those chocolates…

Well, that's a white elephant gift exchange.

Throughout this book, God is inviting you to your own personal gift exchange. But the difference is, God's not trying to pawn off His trash in a pretty wrapper. He wants you to bring whatever's in your backpack and then trade up, big time. He wants you to trade your anxiety for His acceptance. He wants you to trade your past regrets for His future hope. He wants you to trade your grudges for His grace.

And oh, the grudges attach themselves so very easily.

I've had a couple of situations lately where I felt I was treated unfairly. I've spent way too much time rolling that stuff around in my head, focusing on how I was treated by others instead of thinking about how I've been treated by God.

I'm going to live in God's grace. We can trade our guilt for His forgiveness, our despair for His joy, our fear for His promises.

I printed up a little card and put it in my wallet. It contains the words of Isaiah 33:6, which I shared with you earlier in the book, *"[The Lord] will be the sure foundation for your times, a rich store of salvation and wisdom and knowledge; the fear of the Lord is the key to this treasure"* (NIV).

So bring your fear to your Father in heaven, pour your heart out to Him, and then receive His promise. No matter how difficult or easy life is for you right now, you're standing on the edge of incredible because you have the fresh opportunity to abandon your heart to Him and trade up!

Twenty-Two

STEPPING INTO LIFE AND FREEDOM

It may be that you've never taken that step of faith, that you've never begun an intimate, personal, and life-changing relationship with God. You can do it today. It's as simple as realizing that before the creation of the universe, God wanted you to be His daughter or son. He knew we would make mistakes and fall short, that we would be full of fear and even full of sin, that we'd hurt other people and ourselves, that we'd even hurt Him by our attitude.

The Lord knew He had to do something to give us the opportunity for reconciliation with Himself and with each other, so He sent His Son to live a perfect, pure, and holy life and then die on a cross in our place to pay for our sins and mistakes and failures. Because of His great love, we can come to God, and say, "God, forgive me. Help me to make a fresh start."

So if you've never begun a relationship with Him, it's as simple as responding to His call on your life. Jesus said in Matthew 4:17, *"Repent of your sins and turn to God, for the Kingdom of Heaven is near."* The word repent simply means to turn away from selfishness and turn towards God. It means to change your mind and attitude about the Lord, giving Him priority over your life and future.

Repentance is not a jail cell meant to lock you away from freedom and life. It's a key to release you from everything that has held you back from truly living!

Yes, the Kingdom of God is very near to you today. It's as close as the air you're breathing, as intimate as the oxygen circulating in your veins at this very moment.

For those of us who have been walking with God for some time, I want to remind you that the evil one is always trying to add things to your backpack. He's always trying to rob you of your freedom in Christ. 1 Peter 5:8–9 puts it this way: *"Stay alert! Watch out for your great enemy, the devil. He prowls around like a roaring lion, looking for someone to devour. Stand firm against him, and be strong in your faith."*

As we walk through this life, it can be natural to become full of fear, bitterness, uncertainty, or anxiety. But today we have the opportunity for the most fantastic gift exchange of our lives: we can come to God with whatever's in our backpacks, lay it at His feet, and receive His promise of freedom, forgiveness, and life.

I want you to know that the gift exchange we talked about in the last chapter is now open and you're invited to trade up.

Are you still carrying a heavy backpack? I invite you to seek His face. You can go to the cross and kneel before God. Allow Him to take the weight off your shoulders.

I'm going to pray a prayer over you today, knowing that the Lord has intimate knowledge of each person who will read these words. In fact, I want to invite you to join me across time and space as we pray these words together—not only for ourselves and each other, but on behalf of every single person who will ever hold this book in their hands and read these words:

Heavenly Father, You have reminded us today that it's not all up to us and it never has been. That is such a good thing. It's such a relief to be reminded that we can give ourselves away to You.

Whether we're having the most joyful season of our lives or are so broken-hearted that we don't know how to go on, we can abandon ourselves to You. We can begin to live in the incredible as we live in Your strong arms.

Lord, I pray Your grace and strength over the person reading this book right now. For those who are struggling, give them a picture of that beautiful green field, that place of freedom.

Father, we bring our fear to the foot of Your cross and leave it with You. We ask that You would empower us to live the lives we can only live through Your Spirit's leading.

God, we are weak, but You are strong. We come just as we are and exchange our bitterness for Your love, our anxiety for Your acceptance, our past for Your future. I am so thankful that You are doing this in our lives. In Jesus's name we pray, amen.

Twenty-Three

FORTY-ONE YEARS TO MAKE
A BROKEN HEART WHOLE

On the cold January morning when Dick and Judy Hoyt's first child was born, their lives changed forever. But not in the normal way that becoming a parent changes one's life. Although they were initially elated, that very quickly changed.

Because the umbilical cord had been wrapped around baby Rick's neck during birth, his brain was starved of oxygen during delivery. Within the first year, Rick was diagnosed as a spastic quadriplegic with cerebral palsy. Dick and Judy were told to place him in an institution because, in the words of the doctor, "He will never be more than a vegetable."

Rick's father had never heard the word vegetable applied to a human being before. A sombre and emotionally distant military man, Dick wept uncontrollably as he drove home from the hospital with his young wife and son.

Dick and Judy kept putting one foot in front of the other, though, watching the world through bleary eyes. What other choice did they have?

But one day as baby Rick lay on a blanket on the floor, his parents noticed that he could follow them across the room with his eyes. That was more than enough encouragement for them to start dreaming about his future. They weren't going to walk in fear any longer. They began to take baby steps of faith.

Though he was unable to speak, Judy slowly taught him the alphabet and posted sticky notes around the house, labelling every item so he could increase his mental vocabulary, as well as his reading and language skills.

At eight years old, Rick received a computer that allowed him to communicate with those around him. He used head motions to slowly select one letter at a time on his computer screen. Even through this incredibly challenging process of communication, it became clear that Rick was highly intelligent.

At sixteen years old, Rick attended school with the help of care aids, using his upgraded computer and software to communicate with the world around him. He didn't realize it, but Rick was about to go from simply interacting with the world to actually changing it.

This all began because Rick refused to focus on his struggles. Instead, he considered how he could be a help and encouragement to others.

After reading about a five-mile fundraising race for a lacrosse player who had become paralyzed in a car accident, Rick decided that he wanted to get involved. Think about that for a moment—Rick, himself a spastic quadriplegic with cerebral palsy, was concerned about another person he didn't even know. And he wasn't just emotionally empathetic; he wanted to take action and make a real difference in the life of this former lacrosse player.

Rick quickly invited his dad into the proposal. Together they would "run" the five-mile race, Rick riding in a specially adapted wheelchair and Dick providing the rear-wheel-drive muscle!

Well, this father and son team finished the race in second to last place, and Dick was sore for two weeks afterwards. But as Rick later told his father through his one-letter-at-a-time computer communication, "Dad, when I'm out running, I feel like I'm not even handicapped."

That was all Dad needed to hear.

For almost four decades, father and son ran over a thousand races together, including seventy-two marathons and six Iron Man triathlons. They were even inducted into the USA Triathlon Hall of Fame!

But there was something even more amazing about this dynamic partnership of triumph over adversity. You see, at the age of sixty-three, Dick suffered a major heart attack while training for the Boston Marathon. After having an angioplasty, with three stents inserted, Dick's cardiologist explained that if he hadn't been in such good shape due to all his training, the heart attack would most likely have killed him!

It had been more than forty years since the birth of his disabled son and the incredible heartbreak that had gone with it, but all these years later that same young man allowed Dick's heart to literally be made whole and healthy once again.

Perhaps you're in the middle of a long marathon today. You're feeling the intense pain, even the agony. You wonder if you can keep going. No one seems to notice the price you're paying. Will any of this be worth it?

As Hebrews 10:23–25 says,

Let us hold tightly without wavering to the hope we affirm, for God can be trusted to keep his promise. Let us think of ways to motivate one another to acts of love and good works. And let us not neglect our meeting together, as some people do, but encourage one another, especially now that the day of his return is drawing near.

Dick and Rick's story didn't fully begin the day Rick was born a quadriplegic with cerebral palsy. Their story really began to unfold the day young Rick chose to make a difference in the life of a lacrosse player whose world had been turned upside-down.

As I write these words to you today, I have a question for you. Will you dare to step into the incredible by making a tangible difference in the life of someone else today? What one action will you take in the next twenty-four hours to bring hope to someone, increasing their courage and shrinking their fears as they're reminded that they aren't walking this path alone?

Just like young Rick, you have a unique role to play in someone's life today.

Twenty-Four

$2.1 BILLION

$2.1 billion is a lot of money. Really. A lot.

And this specific amount of money has a specific and unique connection to your life today. Don't believe me? Read on.

Any guesses as to why this specific amount of money is connected to your life? Take a moment and make two or three guesses. If you're drawing a blank, consider these possibilities:

1. It's what you could have in your bank account today if you'd bought $10,000 in Apple stock in 1980.
2. It's what your ex-spouse's divorce lawyer would be trying to get from you if you had bought $10,000 in Apple stock in 1980.
3. It's what your lawyer would be trying to get from your ex-spouse if they had bought $10,000 in Apple stock in 1980.

Actually, it's none of these. Although I guess it could be, for some of you. Who am I to crush the hopes and dreams of divorce lawyers everywhere?

In reality, $2.1 billion is the amount of Colombian drug lord Pablo Escobar's cash that was eaten by rats and other rodents while it was stored in warehouses.

I'm serious this time. $2.1 *billion* was eaten by *rats* while sitting in warehouses on the wrong side of town. Shocking.

But now you're understandably asking me, "Sam, what could that possibly have to do with me?"

Everything!

You see, Pablo Escobar had warehouses full of treasures. But because he kept these treasures locked in the darkness, they couldn't be used to impact the world—and they were eventually destroyed. Their value was lost not only to poor Pablo but to the entire world.

Do you realize that you have a warehouse, too? But it's for the *temporary* storage of your treasures. It's located in your mind and in your heart. Perhaps you aren't yet aware of the treasures you possess there. It could be that you don't have a lot of money, and because of that, you think your warehouse is empty.

But it was author Derick Bingham who wrote, "Some people in this world are so poor, all they have is money."[13] You have treasures *much more valuable* than the money you possess or hope to possess one day.

Society teaches us that our goal in life should be to fill our empty warehouses with money, adoration, pleasure, beauty, houses, cars, and boats. We fill them with everything we think we need to pack our empty and yearning hearts.

But what if real significance is found not by filling our empty warehouses, but by emptying our full ones? Would we dare deplete ourselves of every gift of encouragement we've ever

---

[13] Derick Bingham, *A Voice Full of Money, The Parable of 'The Great Gatsby': A Warning Against Moral Drift* (Greenville, SC: Ambassador-Emerald International, 2001), 5.

received by bestowing those gifts on others? Might we attempt to empty ourselves of love by loving others on the far side of extravagance? We might find that our warehouses fill up faster than we can empty them.

You are made in the image of God, the creative and loving centre of this universe. Just as He is a creator, you have been created to create. Just as He is a lover, you have been created to love.

Don't leave your warehouse locked and abandoned. Don't leave your treasures in the darkness. Don't allow the rats and rodents of fear and faithlessness to destroy the treasures God has instilled in you.

Sure, every investment you make in others won't pay off like one hundred shares of Apple stock, but you will eventually lose a hundred percent of the investments you don't make in others.

You may feel frightened to take your hidden treasures and share them with the world. I really do understand that. But as American blogger Evan Sanders says,

Even if you go for it and it doesn't work out, you still win. You had the courage to chase after your dreams [and God's dreams, too] and that's nothing to be ashamed of. That type of bravery will take you places.[14]

You're on the edge of incredible because of the treasure God has put in your warehouse, not only for your sake but for the sake of those around you. By faith, you can draw these treasures out and invest them in others.

The ideas in this book were sitting in my warehouse until I realized I needed to share them with you. That's why I'm

---

[14] Evan Sanders, *The Better Man Project* (Pennsauken, NJ: BookBaby, 2013).

sitting here with a laptop on my knees, writing these words and thinking about you today.

Yes, I have a unique story to bring to this world, but so do you. What are you doing with the riches God has placed in your heart and mind? God is so gracious that He will even use our broken parts to bring hope to others!

Will you let the rats of fear and faithlessness destroy your treasure? I don't know the exact value of what the Lord has placed in your heart and mind, but I do know this: it's worth much more than $2.1 billion.

Twenty-Five
BRAVERY IS CONTAGIOUS

For many years, I've been walking through open doors into adventurous and sometimes even dangerous situations around the world. Maybe it started out as young adult bravado or out of balance testosterone levels, but I honestly enjoy the thrill of it all.

In my last book, *Ten People*,[15] I shared about the military escort our group was given as we journeyed for five hours along the border of Angola and Namibia. That particular day, soldiers with AK-47s rode in front of and behind us on trucks mounted with machine guns. It was almost identical to the Indiana Jones ride at Disneyland, except for one significant exception: it was real.

It was an adventure I'll never forget.

But if the truth be told, I've also been very frightened and anxious at times, especially as I prepared to go to some far-off land or another where I wouldn't be able to control almost any of my sleeping or waking hours.

---

[15] Sam Rowland, *Ten People You've Never Met Are About to Change Your Life* (Winnipeg, MB: Word Alive Press, 2009).

Over the years, I've shared my hope in Jesus with thousands and thousands of incarcerated men and women in prisons around the world. These events have often been highlights on my ministry schedule, as I would witness God resurrecting broken and lost hearts and filling them with a new love and a new spirit. It's a powerful experience to discern someone's destiny being taken apart and reassembled by the Lord.

Well, you can imagine my discouragement as a spiritual and emotional wet, cold blanket was draped around my shoulders as I prepared for an upcoming outreach in Botswana. I had no idea how it got there, but perhaps I had some idea of who had arranged for it.

At the time I was preparing to serve with Youth for Christ. I was also in partnership with another wonderful organization called Prison Fellowship. Prison outreaches were to be a big part of the upcoming ministry trip, and I had been very excited about it up until that point.

But like a developing kidney stone, I had an initial twinge of pain and fear about theses upcoming outreaches, especially and specifically in the prisons. The original fear, though fleeting, soon became an ongoing and reoccurring thought pattern.

The specificity of one particular scene in my mind really concerned me. I saw myself walking through a Botswana prison with my team, some of whom were walking in front of me while others walked behind. We made our way to the makeshift stage where we would share the gospel. I carried my guitar in one hand and my Bible in the other—

—and then it happened. Suddenly, a prisoner jumped up behind me and plunged a jagged piece of metal into my back on the lower right side, just above my beltline. It was so clear and sharp in my mind that I began to wonder if it was a premonition. Not only that, but it replayed in my mind over a number of days.

Well, I certainly wasn't going to cancel the trip over it, but it sure stole my joy and anticipation for the upcoming ministry.

As I rehearsed songs and ministry talks at home, I decided to take a short break to walk down the street and retrieve our mail. Upon opening our little postal box, I was happy to see a letter from Compassion Canada, an incredible ministry of child sponsorship.

Better yet, the letter was from Prossy, the young Ugandan teenager we were sponsoring. Because Prossy spoke and wrote English very well, her letters didn't need to be translated and we had become quite close. Rita and I had exchanged many letters with her over the years. Though just a small child when we'd come in contact with her, Prossy was now fifteen years old.

She wrote,

> Dear Uncle Sam and Auntie Rita,
>
> It was so good to get your last letter. I have been praying for you as you share the love of Jesus all around the world. I want you to know that I was also recently able to share the love of Jesus with many prisoners when I went to a prison here in Uganda!

As I read those last eight words, something clicked into place in my heart. The chains of fear fell off my soul and the wet, heavy blanket of despair slipped off my shoulders. God had used a fifteen-year-old girl half a world away to slay my giant, and she didn't even know it!

If Prossy could go into the prison to share Jesus, so could I. Suddenly, my whole countenance changed as I anticipated the upcoming trip. I no longer dreaded it; now I absolutely couldn't wait to get going!

Prossy's step of faith to serve God in that prison freed me up to do the same in Botswana. During that particular outreach tour, we went to eight different prisons across the country. I still remember kneeling in the dirt and praying over the broken hearts of people who had come to the front to put their trust in Christ. I especially remember seeing a prison guard in full uniform kneel amongst the prisoners with tears in his eyes, giving his heart to Jesus.

What a privilege it will be one day in eternity to introduce that former prison guard and those former inmates to our dear friend and my hero, the giant slayer named Prossy.

Twenty-Six
THE BIG JUMP

There's one story from my life that I've shared face to face with hundreds of thousands of people in high schools, colleges, and prisons around the world. And now I want to share it with you.

It all started with confusion and fear, but it ended with laughter, intimacy, and anticipation. The confusion part began when I read these words from Jesus, found in Matthew 18:3: *"I tell you the truth, unless you turn from your sins and become like little children, you will never get into the Kingdom of Heaven."*

Now, I don't know a lot, but I do know that when Jesus says "I tell you the truth," I better listen to what's coming next.

That's why I was so confused.

I basically understood the first part about turning away from our sins. Instead of stealing, give. Instead of hating, love. Instead of becoming bitter, forgive. Instead of being afraid, have faith.

The part I didn't get was about becoming like little children. Why would Jesus want me to become like a little child? I'd spent my whole life trying to grow up and become a man!

I asked a number of wise people what Jesus meant when He said we should become like little children. I consulted a number of very thick theological books to see what they had to say on the topic. In the end, I wasn't much further ahead.

That is, until a wonder-filled day two weeks later when I brought my four-year old-daughter Tanaya to a swimming pool.

What I'm about to share changed everything for me. And it will change everything for you, too—if you really want it to.

As we entered the pool area, she said with great excitement, "Daddy, you get in the deep water, 'cause I want to stand on the edge of the pool and I want to _____!"

Can you guess what she wanted to do? Of course you can. She wanted to jump!

She wanted to jump into my arms. She was full of bravado, excitement, and anticipation. She seemed unstoppable.

But as she looked down at me from the edge of the pool, as I held my arms out wide, the reality of the situation hit her: she didn't know how to swim. The water was four feet deep and she was only three and a half feet tall.

She became very, very, very frightened.

"Daddy, I don't know how to swim."

"It's okay, sweetheart," I said. "I've got you!"

"But Daddy, *I don't know how to swim* and the water is *way over my head!*"

"Daddy is gonna catch you. Just trust me and jump!"

Two important questions rolled around in her soul that morning—not just in her head, but in her heart. The most important questions always inhabit the heart. And as she stood on the edge of the pool that day, it was time for her to deal with both.

1. Does my daddy really love me?

2. Is my daddy strong enough to catch me?

As she looked down at me with my arms open wide, she said to herself, *Yes, I know my daddy loves me! He has shown that in so many ways. And yes, I know my daddy is strong enough to catch me. I've seen him do many things that show me how strong he is.*

Suddenly, it didn't matter how deep the water was. It didn't even matter whether she could swim. All that mattered were two things: *My daddy loves me and he's strong enough to catch me.*

With a squeal of delight, she jumped off the edge of the pool, flying through the bright blue sky and into my waiting arms. She giggled with joy and relief as she exuberantly declared for everyone to hear, "Daddy, let's do it again!"

And so she jumped again. And again. And again. And each time her faith increased. She asked if I would take a few steps further back from the edge to increase the excitement. Of course, I happily obliged.

She had been so afraid initially that it took her almost ten minutes to jump that first time. But imagine if she had never jumped at all. Imagine if I had kept reaching out to her, waiting for her to jump for twenty minutes, sixty minutes, an hour and a half, and eventually the lifeguards blew the whistle to signal that the swimming session was over. I would have gotten out of the pool, taken my little girl by the hand, and walked with her towards the change rooms.

What if she'd said, "Daddy, I'm ready to jump now"?

With a heavy heart, I would have responded, "Sweetheart, it's too late. I was in the pool calling you with my arms open wide for almost ninety minutes, but you were focused on your inability to swim instead of my ability to catch you. And now it's too late. The pool is closed."

That would have been heartbreaking for me as a father.

I don't want our Father in heaven to experience that heartbreak over you or me, or anyone else.

That morning at the pool, I discovered what Jesus meant when He said we should become like little children. He wants us to become like my daughter, trusting her father and jumping into his arms. It's not about how deep the water is or whether we can swim. The only two questions that matter are: does my Father in heaven really love me, and is He strong enough to catch me?

John 3:16–17 says,

> For this is how God loved the world: He gave his one and only Son, so that everyone who believes in him will not perish but have eternal life. God sent his Son into the world not to judge the world, but to save the world through him.

God sent Jesus because of His tender and yet very powerful love for you! His love overpowers our hopelessness, sinfulness, selfishness, and brokenness. Nothing can ever separate you from His powerful love for you. He gave His only Son to die in our place, paying the price for our transgressions, so we could be lavished with forgiveness, hope, and a restored relationship with our Father in heaven.

So the answer to the first question—does my Father in heaven really love me?—is answered in the person of Jesus. Yes! Yes! Yes!

And how about the second question—is He strong enough to catch you? This is another way of asking, "Can I really trust Him with my life?" Well, if God is strong enough to create billions of stars and planets and scatter them across the universe, then He's certainly strong enough to catch you and me.

I don't want to spend my life standing on the edge of the swimming pool, filled with fear, focusing on my own shortcomings and wondering what could have been. I want to focus on my Father in heaven, trusting that He loves me and is strong enough to catch me. I'm jumping into His arms again by writing these words to you today. And when tomorrow morning comes, I'm gonna shout out for the whole pool to hear, "Daddy, let's do it again!"

Matthew 10:39 says, *"If you cling to your life, you will lose it; but if you give up your life for me, you will find it."* When I read these words, I think about two things. I think about my daughter at the swimming pool, all those years ago, and I think about you, right now.

Twenty-Seven

HIS NAME IS DAVID

We can rejoice, too, when we run into problems and trials, for we know that they help us develop endurance. And endurance develops strength of character, and character strengthens our confident hope of salvation. (Romans 5:3–4)

Have you ever seen a Bible verse in a book or magazine and just sort of skipped over it, possibly because you kind of knew the verse already and you wanted to get to the good stuff in the book? Well, on this day and on this page, as you read these words, I want you to know that Romans 5:3–4 *is* the good stuff.

That's why I'm putting it down here for you to read again—not to skip over, but to let it soak into your soul. I encourage you to read the next thirty-four words slowly and with great intent, like your inner joy depends on it.

We can rejoice, too, when we run into problems and trials, for we know that they help us develop endurance. And endurance develops strength of character, and character strengthens our confident hope of salvation. (Romans 5:3–4)

You have the opportunity to rejoice today—if you want to. And not because everything is going so well, but perhaps because it isn't going so well. God is just as much the God of the not-going-so-well days as He is of the most perfect day you can imagine.

The question is this: do you place more value on having the perfect day or do you place more value on walking with the God of the great days, the heart-breaking days, and the somewhere-in-between days?

The hard things you're facing right now will help you develop endurance. That newly developed endurance will create strength of character in your innermost parts. That robust character will nourish your confident hope of salvation. That confident hope, as deep and intimate as the marrow in your bones right now, changes everything.

How do I know? Because David is a friend of mine.

And I'd really like to introduce you to him, but that just isn't going to happen. No, David isn't an imaginary friend. He's my real friend. Truth be told, he's one of my best friends.

He just doesn't live on this earth anymore.

He left last month. The last time I saw David was seventy-two hours before he packed his bags and left.

Funny thing, though... he left all that luggage behind.

I walked into the hospice ward of Peace Arch Hospital, having just gotten a call that David had been moved there. If I wanted to see him, today would be the day.

My courage and faith received a turbocharge as I sat with my friend, who was only three days away from stepping into eternity. He was joyful, fearless, forgiven, and free. He didn't dwell on the past but anticipated the future. He was fully alive, not denying the realities of his situation, but focusing on a grander reality.

Jesus's sacrifice on the cross and His resurrection from the dead had changed *everything* for David. What a miracle. What an example of courage and faith for us to follow!

"Sam, how is the writing going for your new book, *On the Edge of Incredible*?" he asked.

"I'm right in the middle of it, and I'm pretty encouraged."

"Sam," he whispered with a glint in his eye. He motioned for me to come closer. "I'm on the edge of incredible right now!"

One of the greatest gifts God has ever given me was that fifteen minutes with David Fearon. I was given an insight into a man's soul as he was preparing to leave this world, and that insight was glorious! If he could be so full of joy and anticipation and freedom in that situation, what could possibly stop you and me from living on the edge of incredible in our own situations, however difficult they may be?

What was it that gave David this supernatural peace and the incredible ability to look forward with great joy, even in the face of his own death? It can all be summed up in these forty words:

> ... [I am] no longer counting on being saved by being good enough or by obeying God's laws, but by trusting Christ to save me; for God's way of making us right with himself depends on faith—counting on Christ alone. (Philippians 3:9, TLB)

You see, if being right with God depends on us being good enough, how will we ever know if we've made it? How can we live with peace if we're always one screw-up away from being rejected? We can't! That's why we need to have a personal encounter with the creator of the universe, who says,

Can a mother forget her nursing child? Can she feel no love for the child she has borne? But even if that were possible, I would not forget you! See, I have written your name on the palms of my hands. (Isaiah 49:15–16)

What else does the Lord say to you? He says, *"I have loved you, my people, with an everlasting love. With unfailing love I have drawn you to myself"* (Jeremiah 31:3).

With unfailing love, He is drawing you to Himself, even now.

Ultimately, if you could know with certainty that your past mistakes, sins, and selfish choices have been completely forgiven and covered over with deep love and unlimited acceptance, wouldn't that free you up to live in a new way? Additionally, if you discovered that your future was guaranteed to include unrestrained and unending intimacy with your creator, wouldn't that give you a boost of courage during the tough times? Finally, if you knew that you were steadily moving towards more life, beauty, and freedom than you are currently able to comprehend, wouldn't that change your perception of yourself and the life you have ahead of you, even the life beyond this world?

The creator of this universe didn't just make the beautiful beaches of Hawaii, the majestic alpine mountains of Switzerland, and the beautiful waters of the Zambezi River as it roars over the cliffs of Victoria Falls in Zimbabwe.

He made you.

And you are more important and precious to Him than all of these other wonders of the world.

Many years ago, He gave His only Son to die on a cross, paying the penalty for all our sins and selfishness. Jesus's death satisfied the justice of the universe, so that as we come to God with humble and sincere hearts and ask for forgiveness and a new start, we can truly receive it.

Have you received this forgiveness and everlasting love? Are you living in the midst of it now? You certainly can be, but you have to want it more than anything else.

I shared earlier in the book that Jesus said in Matthew 10:39, *"If you cling to your life, you will lose it; but if you give up your life for me, you will find it."* I urge you to give up your own life and present it to the Lord. He will take it and do something beautiful with it.

Paul Ciniraj, a missionary in India, penned the beautiful words of this poem:

> A basketball in my hands is worth about $19.
> A basketball in Michael Jordan's hands is worth
> about $33 million.
> It depends on whose hands it's in...
>
> A baseball in my hands is worth about $6.
> A baseball in Mark McGuire's hands is worth $19
> million.
> It depends on whose hands it's in...
>
> A rod in my hands will keep away a wild animal.
> A rod in Moses' hands will part the mighty sea.
> It depends on whose hands it's in...
>
> A sling shot in my hands is a toy.
> A slingshot in David's hands is a mighty weapon.
> It depends on whose hands it's in...

Two fish and five loaves in my hands is
a couple of fish sandwiches.
Two fish and five loaves in Jesus' hands will feed
thousands.
It depends on whose hands they're in ...

Nails in my hands might produce a bird house.
Nails in Christ Jesus' hands will produce salvation
for the entire world.
It depends on whose hands they're in ...

As you see now it depends on whose hands it's in.
So put your concerns, worries, fears, hopes, dreams,
families and relationships in God's Hands.
Because, It depends on whose hands they're in.[16]

At this moment, you might be asking yourself, *Well, what will happen with my life if I trust God with it or if I hold onto it myself?* Great news! I can give you the answer to that question right now with one hundred percent accuracy: it all depends on whose hands it's in.

As John 1:12–13 says,

But to all who believed him and accepted him, he gave the right to become children of God. They are reborn—not with a physical birth resulting from human passion or plan, but a birth that comes from God.

Have you received Jesus into the centre of your soul? Have you welcomed Him into the deepest parts of your heart and

---

[16] Paul Ciniraj, "It All Depends on Whose Hands It's In," *Paul Ciniraj.* December 28, 2010 (https://siniraj.wordpress.com/2010/12/28/it-all-depends-on-whose-hands-its-in/).

mind and life? If not, you can do that right now through a beautiful step of faith, a step that will move you from the edge of incredible right into the very centre of it.

It's as simple as talking with God, from your heart to His heart.

You can share these words with the Lord and find more life, acceptance, forgiveness, and freedom than you ever thought possible:

> Dear Jesus, I am turning to You with all that I am. Make a beautiful change in my heart and in my mind. I am no longer counting on being saved by being good enough or by obeying laws, but by trusting You alone to save me. Forgive me for my sins and selfishness. Thank You for paying the price for my forgiveness on the cross. Help me to follow You all the days of my life. Help me to love You and to love others in the same way You have loved me. In Jesus's name I pray, amen.

Jesus knows you, and if you've put your trust in Him and received Him into the centre of your soul, now you know Him, too! This is not the end of the story, but the beginning—the beginning of an intimate journey through life, hand in hand with your creator.

One day we will all stand on the edge of incredible in the same way my friend David did that day in the hospice ward. And even on that day, what Jesus did for you will be a rock-solid foundation for your life. And for your eternity.

Twenty-Eight
FACING OUR OWN LE MORNE

It was a Thursday evening like any other. With only a few days left until Christmas, Rita and I were anticipating a wonderful celebration with four generations of our family.

But life had other plans.

Rita had made a delicious homemade pizza for dinner that night. I ate a bit too much and enjoyed it thoroughly. I was still basking in the warm glow of that pizza as I drifted off to sleep, not knowing that my body would wake me ninety minutes later and my life would be forever changed.

I awoke suddenly and very uncomfortably. I couldn't put my finger on what exactly was going on, but everything felt off. I was very anxious, which was highly unusual for me. There was a burning in my throat and a feeling of intense pressure in my neck as well as a general tightness in the whole upper part of my body.

I didn't realize it then, but I was in the middle of a heart attack.

Over the next few days in the hospital, reality began setting in. I had three blocked arteries, including one of the major ones, the one nicknamed "the widowmaker." I awaited an angioplasty to try to reopen the blockages and repair the damage.

I felt very much like I imagine the slaves of Mauritius felt on that day long ago as they stood on the cliffs of Le Morne, watching the police coming towards them. Full of dread and discouragement, I wondered if there was any future for me on this planet.

Cancelling upcoming ministry tours across Hungary, Zimbabwe, and Ukraine, I wondered if I would ever again have the privilege of sharing my faith and hope in Jesus with young people around the world as I had done over the last twenty-five years.

Again, like the Mauritian slaves, I felt hopeless. Was I staring into the face of death, or at least the death of life as I knew it?

A giant brick had been thrown through the middle of my ideal stained-glass window and now I had a choice to make. Would I succumb to despair or anger, shouting out, "Look what life has done to me"?

I admit that I definitely had some moments of discouragement, anger, and disbelief at my completely unforeseen situation. I also felt a sense of loss. Not only wasn't I able to travel the globe, I wasn't even able to drive my car for a while after the medical procedures were completed.

And so I said to the Lord, "Father, I've got a broken heart. Literally, a broken heart. And the broken pieces of my hopes and dreams, the broken pieces of my life, feel like the broken pieces of the stained-glass window that used to be my life. But You're the Father of creativity. Would You take these broken pieces and make something beautiful out of them? It may not be what I had in mind, and that's okay. If You're willing to take these broken pieces of mine, Lord, then I freely give them to You."

It was pretty clear to me what I was losing because of this situation, but I had to step out in faith to trust the Lord for what I might be gaining, even if it was beyond my ability to touch it, see it, or even imagine it.

On a new journey now, I simply put one foot in front of the other as I try to trust the Lord. I am beginning to realize that most of the control I thought I possessed before was just a fantasy. There is actually something refreshing about realizing at the core of my being that my life is in the hands of my Saviour.

If my Papa in heaven chooses to give me thirty-five more years on this earth, that's fantastic. But if it all ends later this week, it will still be incredible, because either way, I get to be in His strong arms.

That thought generates a lot of peace. It's almost like a stream of living water that keeps bubbling up from the deepest part of my soul.

In this season, I'm finding out that God can do more with the broken pieces of my life than I could have ever done with them, even if I'd had everything exactly the way I wanted it to be.

As a result of having to cancel or postpone my overseas travel schedule, I've had the opportunity to write this book for you. And for that, I will forever be thankful.

EPILOGUE

Real healing will start taking place when we become more connected to what *could be* and less connected to what *has been*.

I love that. I love that for you. I love that for me, too, because the Lord has healed many of my wounds. I've also seen Him do this in the lives of countless other people around the world.

Yes, we'll probably retain many of the scars. And yes, we may even walk with a limp for the rest of our lives. But that scar or limp shouts out to the universe that we haven't only survived what could have destroyed us, but we're thriving and creating and reflecting beauty and life everywhere we go.

As you choose to respond to your life and current circumstances with a leap into faith instead of a leap into fear, there's no telling how it will positively affect not only your life but the lives of so many around you.

Think about Dick Hoyt, whose leap of faith with his disabled son Rick eventually saved his life when a heart attack hit. Think about Wilma in Namibia, whose leap into faith allowed her to create beauty instead of bitterness. Think of the newly freed Mauritian slaves who chose a leap into fear. Their only enduring legacy is of how *not* to face our fears and the things that break our hearts. Compare their fear-based response to the faith-based response of David Fearon, who, while facing certain death, was full of joy and hope and anticipation! Those few moments I spent with David in the hospital will continue to inspire me for the rest of my life.

As I've spent time with and studied tens of thousands of people of all socioeconomic levels and from dozens of countries around the world, I've noticed something life-changing. It's not how many possessions, how much status, how much beauty, or even how much power a person has that gives them an ultimate sense of joy, hope, and self-worth. In fact, it's not something on the outside at all. It's something unseen. It's a miracle, a gift, something only God can give us.

Living in the incredible doesn't mean a life free of pain, heartache, and disappointment. These things will come our way no matter what. Living in the incredible means living, laughing, loving, and serving today, even amid all the difficulties.

You might be going through some very deep water right now. You might feel too exhausted to swim against the tide. But catch a fresh glimpse of your Father in heaven as you're reminded of these words from Romans 12:3: *"The only accurate way to understand ourselves is by what God is and by what he does for us, not by what we are and what we do for him"* (MSG).

Suddenly, it doesn't matter how deep the water is. It doesn't even matter whether you can swim or not. All that matters are two things: our Father loves you and He is strong enough to catch you.

"Daddy, let's do it again!"

ABOUT THE AUTHOR

Sam Rowland is a speaker, author, and musician. He has shared his story and music with the tribal peoples of Namibia, Africa. The secret police came to every concert he performed in Myanmar in Southeast Asia. His songs have stirred the hearts of people in the jungle hills of Jamaica in the West Indies. He has opened his heart unashamedly to share his journey in great cities and little villages all across the European continent. Concert and speaking tours have taken him from coast to coast in both the United States and in his home and native land of Canada.

By weaving together humour, music, and thought-provoking insights, Sam has impacted thousands of people on five continents. He has also recorded six CDs as well as a DVD called *Words & Music... Live from Europe.*

Sam and his wife Rita live in Vancouver, British Columbia, Canada. They have four grown children and an ever-growing number of grandkids.

Dear Reader,

We would like to hear from you!

If this book has encouraged or impacted you, please contact us at sam@youthunlimited.com or through our website at www.samrowland.org and share your story with us.

We look forward to hearing from you.

Requests for information should be addressed to:

Sam Rowland
c/o Youth Unlimited
#115-12975 84th Avenue
Surrey, BC
Canada V3W 1B3
E-mail: sam@youthunlimited.com
Website: www.samrowland.org